Traditional Recipes of

GREEK
Cooking

The Best
Traditional Recipes of
GREEK
Cooking

221 RESIPES

THE GREEK DIET THROUGHOUT THE AGES

THE OLIVE AND OIL IN GREECE

THE GREEK CHEESE

GREEK WINES

INDEX

EDITIONS HAITALIS

The Best
Traditional Recipes of
GREEK
Cooking

Copyright © 2002 Editions Haitalis

ISBN: 960-8284-14-7

Editing and DTP: Barrage Ltd

Texts: Maria Mavromataki

Art Editing: Fotini Svarna

Colour seperations: Haitalis

Printing: Lithografiki S.A.

Photographs: Haitalis Publishing Co. archive

Published by: Haitalis
13, ASTROUS ST., 13121 ATHENS, GREECE
Tel: 010 5766.883 - Fax: 010 5729.985

CONTENTS

A FEW WORDS
FROM THE EDITOR

If someone wants to describe the variety, flavour and savour of the Greek cuisine, they will have to fill page after page. Moreover, many have sung the Greek recipes' praises. The purpose of this book is completely different. We have tried to include the most representative recipes of the Greek cuisine as well as all the special dishes of the Greek areas.

All these original recipes have been written clearly and accurately. Therefore, if you follow the instructions faithfully, your success will be guaranteed providing your guests with wonderful tasty experiences.

On the other hand, this book has also some other ambitions. We have tried to include a small piece of Greece. To include the saltiness of the Aegean islands, the fragrance of thyme and oregano of the Peloponnese and Sterea Ellada (Central Greece), the attractive delicacies from Macedonia and Thrace, the sweet yearning of Crete, Rhodes and Corfu.

Our other ambition, therefore, is to remind you through the recipes of the beautiful moments you have lived in some Greek corner; the beautiful landscapes you have seen, the specialties you have tasted and, of Cupid, the winged God of Love, you have met one night, somewhere on a deserted beach. Because all of us nurture these nostalgic memories. All these have surely whetted your appetite. So, let's go! Tuck up your sleeves, choose the recipe you prefer and... enjoy your meal!

THE FOUR SEASONS OF THE GREEK CUISINE

The Greek housewife today —wife, mother and, more recently, working woman- is the direct, modern descendant of the goddess of antiquity, Hestia, protector of family peace and happiness. Therefore, as a descendant of the goddess, the Greek woman knows well that love starts from the heart but goes down to the stomach and stays there. This is the reason why she is so much involved with cooking in such an artful way. Every season of the year, offering her different products, is a new challenge for her to ensure her cooking abilities and her inexhaustible imagination. Moreover, the Greek calendar with its numerous official and semi-official celebrations gives her the chance to practice her art and keep the traditions alive by practicing the traditionally long established Greek recipes.

bringing not only fun and fancy dresses but also invitations to meals inspiring the hostess with new, wonderful creations. During this period, the leading place in the Greek cuisine belongs to meat with pasta, pork -cooked in numerous different ways- and tasty pastry, such as honey puffs (loukoumades) and xirotigana.

The productive imagination of the Greek woman even managed to overcome the big trial of Lent. Despite the restrictions imposed by religious tradition and the few kinds of food which are allowed, she is able to create fantastic delicacies and even Lenten pastry.

Seafood, roe egg salad (taramosalata), tzatziki, spinach pie and all the other kinds of vegetable pies made the Greek cuisine famous all over the world.

Then comes Easter. During this period, the top position belongs to the lamb, the kid and the well known mayiritsa, Midnight Easter soup.

Starting from the Christmas and New Year holiday periods, the Greek housewife, after establishing her self in her personal "kingdom'"-her kitchen- begins preparing the traditional Greek pastry. Short bread cookies (kourambiedes), small honey cakes (melomakarona), sweet pleats (diples), New Year cakes (vassilopites) and New Year cookies are found in every house during the holiday season.

As soon as the New Year preparations finish, the Carnival comes

On Easter Sunday, the traditional spit is set up in all the houses, while during the following days there is a huge variety of meals based on lamb or kid meat; in the oven with potatoes or pasta, in the pot, fricassee, grilled steaks and many others. Of course it would be a big omission not to mention what gives the Greek Easter an original colour: red eggs.

And at last summer is here; the golden Greek summer. For our country, summer means fruit and vegetables. Plenty of fresh fruit, which for many people replace a normal meal during the period of excessive heat. Other times, they become tasty preserves, marmalades, and jams in order to be consumed in the coming winter. As far as the vegetables (okras, string beans, courgettes, aubergi-nes) are concerned, they are the basis for most of summer foods. Among the different types of fried food, vegetable dishes or other dishes, the top

position belongs to the well-known and tasty moussaka. And when autumn comes, the first cold will bring to the kitchen the original Greek bean soup.

This book is, therefore, another invitation to a meal which exploits the four seasons of the Greek cuisine. It offers you the opportunity to enrich your knowledge about the culinary art and excite your beloved ones when you present them with the special products of the Greek land prepared in such an exquisite way.

INVITATION TO A MEAL

Nature endowed Greece with a bright sun, wonderful sea and rich soil. The combination of these three elements offers a big variety of products of superb quality which manage to meet even the most difficult demands in taste. Which are, though, the special factors which have given the Greek cuisine the special position it occupies by right and guarantee the esteem of everybody that knows it?

The main reason for this supremacy is of course the big variety of ingredients used for the preparation of a meal. The Greek soil generously offers its products every season of the year -pure and tasty products which are an inexhaustible spring of culinary inspiration. Maintaining the traditional way in animal breeding and fruit and vegetable cultivation is the best guarantee for the quality, food value and savour of the Greek dishes -even for their good aesthetic presentation.

On the other hand, the hospitable feelings of the Greeks, who have remained faithful to Xenios Zeus, decisively contribute to the success of the Greek cuisine.

Hospitality, the generous giving to the stranger, the cordial treat transform the simple art of cooking into an art of communication and reconciliation. In this light, even the scantiest table acquires an unrivalled taste and quality when accompanied by a cozy atmosphere and a good company. And, of course in this field, the Greeks are the best.

Their biggest secret, however, is the long established through the centuries, continuous tradition of culinary art. The Greek woman owes her cooking skills to the heritage of her ancestors, the "experience" of three thousand years, which allows her to create true tasty miracles. Since the first stages of their culture, the Greeks have never neglected the quality of their foods and drinks.

Their mythology and history are full of examples of rich dishes cooked with artistry and imagination. Either in peace or war, in celebrations, in joy or grief, on any occasion the special guest was always culinary pleasure. The request of the Olympian Gods was similar: they were appeased with the fragrance of roasted meat from the sacrificed animals as it ascended towards the sky. Even philosophy was connected with taste in ancient times.

Philosophers postulated their theories during the famous symposia enjoying special dishes and wines. Even today a good meal is often accompanied by spiritual queries of every kind.

So, cooking always carried special importance for the Greeks. Worshippers of beauty, they did not think of it only as a necessary procedure for their daily diet but as a means for satisfying the sense of taste, exciting their creative imagination and expressing some of their artistic worries.

The preparation of meals could possibly be defined as a kind of art; an art ready at any minute to create a new culinary feast.

The ideogrammatic pictures of (1, the olive tree 2, the olive 3, the oil).

One of the two fishermen who ornament corners of room 5 in the West House - Akrotiri Santorini- (Athens, Nation. Arch. Museum).

1

2

3

THE GREEK DIET
THROUGHOUT THE AGES

THE PREHISTORIC ERA

In prehistoric times, long before man began the cultivation of the land and animal breeding, food was obtained by hunting, fishing and collecting wild fruit. It is known as the "food collection stage", which coincides with the Paleolithic Age. The next stage is the "food producing" one which in Greece starts during the Neolithic Age, in the 7ᵗʰ millennium BC. Man becomes now a farmer cultivating the land to get food and breeding the animals of the area. Of course we do not know the dietary habits of so remote a period but there is enough evidence about cattle raising and cultivations which allows us to come up with some conclusions. It is proven that during the first phases of agricultural development, grains (*wheat, barley, oat, rye*) and legumes (*lentil, peas)* were grown, while the diet was complemented with wild fresh or dried fruit, such as *wild olives, oaks, nuts, plums* and *sloes.* A little later, vine and broad beans cultivation appears and there are findings showing that the fruit of the *fig tree, the wild pear* and *the almond tree* were known. In the same period, the Neolithic man breeds *wild sheep, pigs, cattle* for their meat and milk and is also fed with *fish* and *seafood.*

The information we have on the diet of the Bronze Age (Minoan, Mycenaean, Cycladic) is definitely much more. At that period (3000-1100 BC) the cultivation of the same agricultural products and the breeding of the same animals as before continued. At the same time, though, new cultivations which enriched their diet or new techniques in food processing were developed making the cuisine of that period more refined. This is attested by the

numerous cooking utilities having come to light in excavations (kneading-troughs, millstones, mortars, pots, bowls, plates, cups, gourds, spoons, knives, spits, storing large jars etc) but also by the fruit found charred in the remains of the palaces. Cooking was done in special ovens outside the main house and the meal was served on wooden or stone benches. But, as it appears there were no specific meal times and they ate whenever they felt hungry.

Vegetables and legumes held the first place in the diet of the period. *Lentils, chickpeas, broad beans, split peas, artichokes, beet roots, marrows, turnips, cucumbers, celery* were served boiled or grilled or some of them, raw. Most of the dishes acquired a particular taste with the addition of multifarious spices such as *oregano, mint, thyme, saffron, garlic, clove* and *caper,* while some herbs used to make medic-inal herb teas (*sage, mint, dittany)* were known too. The main ingredient of the diet was of course *wheat.* They made flour, the basic ingredient of *porridge* and of many types of *pies* which they sprinkled with honey and sesame or even (in Crete) with poppy seeds, by grinding wheat as well as barley. They also made *bread* from flour which very often they offered for worship purposes at sanctuaries.

Olives and *olive oil* were always part of the daily menu. But apart from olive oil, flavoured oil from *sesame, clove* and *flax* was also used. Linseed oil was used

p. 17
A jug with breast-like protruberances painted with ears of barley from Akrotiri -Santorini (Athens Archaeological Museum).

p.18
A wooden panel from Pitsia near Corinth showing a sacrificial scene (540 BC, Athens Archaeological Museum).

p. 19
A black-figure cylix. Dionysus is shown as a carefree voyager drinking wine from a horn. A vine covered with grapes has sprung from the mast of the ship, and there are dolphins swimming in the sea (540-530 BC, Munich Archaeological Collection).

to oil grilled pies. Some dried fruit, such as *almonds, chickpeas, acorns, walnuts* and *locust beans* were also known. Moreover, they used to extract a special sweetener, *locust bean* honey, from locust beans which they put in their sweets together with honey from bees. There were also a big variety of fruits: *figs, grapes, pears, sloes, plums, quince, apples* and *loquats*. Citrus trees were completely unknown.

There was also a big variety in kinds of meat. *Pork, beef, lamb and kid meat* was eaten grilled, boiled or finely cut in pies. *Milk* and *cheese* were also usual products, while *hens* were bred for their meat and eggs as well as *pigeons*. Hunting, a usual occupation of the prehistoric era, brought tasty delicacies to the daily menu, such as *wild boars, deer, roe, wild goat, hares* and *wild bulls*. The fact as well that at least in Crete *snails* were particularly popular is quite interesting. Minoans used to collect them from the fields in such quantities that a big amount was exported to foreign markets. On the other hand, fishing enriched their diet with many kinds of fish and sea food: *sea bream, red mullet, tuna, grouper, scorpion fish, gray mullet, stingray, bass fish, sardine, gilthead, octopus, cuttlefish* and others which were consumed grilled, salted or sun dried or in soups. Of course, the drink that was served with every kind of food was *wine* which was plentiful in every region of Greece.

THE CLASSIC ERA

Many elements of the prehistoric diet are found in the classic era during which cooking became a kind of art. For the first time during the 5th century BC, special attention was paid to the creation of tasty food and many cooks, interested in creating the so called "mixtures", that is interested in gastronomy, were distinguished.

During the 4th century BC, the first cookbook was written in Sicily by Archestratos. The information we have, though, today comes from another writer, Atheneos, who, in his work "Dipnosophistes", (Sophists of Symposia), describes the process of cooking from the Homeric era up to the 2nd century AD. In his book all the kinds of usual foods, their names and the way of preparation are mentioned attesting the wealth of the Greek dishes and their importance for the consequent development of cooking up to modern times. Many of the modern Greek dishes originate from ancient times; therefore, it is obvious that in the basic core there has been a continuity of the Greek cuisine for thousand years.

A basic type of food of the ancient

Greeks as well as all the ancient peoples is *soup*. The famous *"kykeon"* of the antiquity was nothing more than a nourishing porridge made of barley, which was used for religious reasons as well. They often added mashed legumes and vegetables or pieces of meat, of poultry and fish. *"Melas zomos"*, which was the main food of the Spartans, was a soup made of pork, blood and vinegar.

Cereals, which were cultivated in big quantities, were the basic ingredients for many dishes. *Wheat or barley flour* was used in the preparation of the so-called "plakountes". *Plakountes* were small pies in different shapes which were roasted and sprinkled with honey, walnuts, and almonds or sometimes with sweet cheese. They also used to make a big variety of *bread* using flour (wheat or barley) in different shapes (round, square, wide etc) and cooked in different ways (in the oven, on the grate, in a vessel floating in water). Other ingredients were often mixed with flour, such as *honey, oil, wine* and *spices*. The *"popana"*, special round small bans, were offered on the shrines during ceremonies while big loaves of bread were offered to the Gods during the celebrations of Thesmoforia (in honour of Demeter, the goddess, celebrations for the fertility of women and the soil), Thargilia (15/5-15/6, celebrating harvesting) and Thalysia (in honour of Demeter and Dionysus). They made

groats (crushed grains), which replaced rice, from wheat ground in hand-mills. Our ancestors did not have any rice, but they knew of its existence as a dish of the East. Finally, they used to make pastry sheet (*fyllo*) for pastry filling wrapped in dough. This filling often included almonds, walnuts, sesame and honey and was similar to the modern baklava, which therefore is of Greek origin and not Turkish as it is wrongly believed.

The most popular dishes of the antiquity included of course legumes and vegetables. Some of them were consumed raw and others boiled or roasted. In special celebrations (Anthestiria [in honour of Dionysus], Thargilia),

the ancient Greeks gathered a small quantity from all kinds of legumes and vegetables cultivated by them, boiled everything together and offered them to the Gods to thank them for the fertility of the soil. After the celebration, all the family gathered around the table and ate from the so-called *polyspermia (multi grains)*. This ceremony shows the importance of the soil products for their diet. The most popular legumes were *lentils, broad beans, peas, chick-*

p. 20
Fruit stand and vessels of Kamares ware, dating from c.1800 BC. (Irakleio Archaeological Museum - Room III)

p. 21
View of the western storehouses, with their storage jars. Among the jars, rows of square tanks which were lined with alabaster plaques can be seen. Knossos-Crete.

peas, horse beans and lupines, whereas they used many kinds of vegetables and wild herbs (*onions, courgettes, cabbage, mallows, artichokes, chicories etc*). The ancient Greeks did not know of the existence of tomatoes and potatoes, of course, two basic vegetables of the modern cuisine. However, they loved spices, which added a spicy taste to their food (*oregano, saffron, thyme, pepper, clove etc*). In ancient times there was a big preference for strong but mixed tastes as well (sour, sweet and salty altogether). One of the spiciest dishes was a sauce made of garlic and oil, something like the modern *skordalia* (garlic paste). They also used mustard grains, which today are the basis for mustard, as a spice. As far as fruit are concerned, there was always a big variety available: *grapes, apples* in 25 species (they used to make cider from apples), *cherries, pears, quinces* (they ate them boiled and during the Roman era they were served with meat), *pomegranates* -symbol of fertility- (the juice of unripe pomegranate was, due to the lack of lemons, the basic source of sour taste for food), *figs* (fresh or dried).

Dried figs, almonds, roasted chickpeas and *walnuts* were called "*tragemata*" which accompanied wine drinking after the main dishes during symposia.

The meat and poultry consumed were not very different from the ones of the prehistoric era.

Pork was the most popular type of meat and it also had a sacred importance since it was considered to be the symbol of fertility and was offered to the Gods. *Lamb* and *kid* were mainly eaten roasted on the spit and from their intestines they used to make "*eilito*" something similar to the modern *garduba* and *kokoretsi*. Of course there was *beef* meat and *chicken meat* as well. Eggs, at least during the Roman era, were fried, boiled or cooked mixed with *milk* and *honey* in a form of a cream which thickened when put over fire. Another popular dish was *game,* as well as *meat pies,* the so-called "*artokreata*". However, meat was not consumed on an everyday basis but on exceptional occasions, mainly after sacrifices.

On the contrary, *fish* was particularly popular and was either grilled or boiled. *Fish soup* occupied a special place: it was prepared in a big pot, "*kakavi*", from which the modern word for fish soup made of a big variety of fish -"kakavia"- is derived. Quite often, fish was kept salted, mainly *sardines, common mackerels* and *bonitos* and were known with the name "*tarichos*". From the intestines of the fish they used to make "*garos*", a kind of sauce used not only for fish recipes but for meat and vegetable recipes as well. *Mollusks* and *shellfish* were also popular, mainly *cuttlefish* and *octopuses*. In general, it seems that in ancient times many kinds of fish and sea food were known, perhaps many more than the ones we know today.

THE ROMAN- BYZANTINE-MODERN ERA

The ancient Greek cuisine provided the Roman one with many of its characteristic elements. The Romans appreciated the cooking abilities of the Greeks early on and asked the best cooks of the time for advice on their meals. When the Roman Empire spread to the then known world, it was decisively influenced by the diet habits of the enslaved peoples and, having the financial ability to import the most peculiar and expensive products, it created a complex cuisine. The luxurious Roman banquets and the famous "*Lucullean feasts*" remained in history for their wealth and eccentricity. Gradually, though, the tendency of the Romans for recherchè dishes brought satiety and led their cuisine to degeneration and fall. The Byzantine world, which followed the Roman one, quickly returned to the ancient Greek tradition of cooking and developed it assimilating the influences of the diet of the sub-

jects of the Empire in a creative way.

During the Turkish domination, the Greeks borrowed many elements from the Turkish cuisine which in its turn had already borrowed many elements of the Greek cuisine from the Byzantines. The new loans from the Turks, as well as from the Venetians and the French, who had taken possession of some Greek territories, were easily adjusted to the traditional tasty habits. In modern times, the development of tourism brought the European cuisine closer to Greece providing new culinary choices, unknown in the past. The cooking of Eastern countries and Latin American ones has been widely spread in recent years while the American cuisine, a mirror of the modern way of life, tends to be imposed all over the world. Although cultural exchanges are welcomed in any field, the culinary internationalism prevailing today threatens to lead to extinction many original Greek traditional recipes. Let us hope that the wealth of the Greek cuisine, its long standing tradition and the nourishing value of its products will constitute the biggest guarantee for the preservation of our national cooking heritage.

p.22 Hades was not only the terrible god of the Underworld, he was also a life-giving deity whose task it was to prepare the fruits for growth beneath the earth. On the red-figure pelike of this illustration he is holding a horn from which he is scattering seed across a ploughed field. (430-420 BC, Athens Archaeological Museum).

Appetizers

- *Small Cheese Pies*

- *Giant Beans with Sausages*

- *Spinach and Cheese Pies*

Tyropitákia

SMALL CHEESE PIES

Melt half the butter in a pot. Stir in the flour and mix well with the help of a spatula for about 5 minutes. Add the warmed milk stirring all the time to avoid its lumping. Remove from heat; add the feta cheese, crumbled, the nutmeg, the eggs, salt and pepper and let the mixture cool.

Cut the «fyllo» pastry into long strips, about 5 cm (2 inches) wide. Take two strips together and brush all over the surface with the melted butter.

Place a teaspoon of the filling at one end of each strip and fold over into triangles. Place pies in lines on a pan and bake in a medium oven for about 35 minutes (both upper and lower elements of the oven should be lit). Serve the pies either hot or cold.

5 - 6 SERVINGS
◇ ½ kilo (1 lb 2 oz) «fyllo» pastry
◇ 1 teacup flour
◇ 1 teacup butter or margarine
◇ 2 ½ teacups milk
◇ 350 grams (10 oz) feta cheese
◇ 3 eggs
◇ 1 teaspoon nutmeg
◇ Salt-pepper

Kalitsoúnia Krítis

CRETAN SMALL CHEESE PIES

◇ 400-500 grams (14 oz - 1 lb 2 oz) unsalted cheese, e.g. cottage cheese
◇ 1-2 tablespoons mint
◇ 1 egg
◇ 5 tablespoons sugar
◇ 1 glass olive or good vegetable oil for frying
◇ pastry

PASTRY

Add some water and salt to three teacups of flour to make thick dough. Roll out the dough and cut round shapes with a pastry cutter or a glass.

FILLING

Mix the cheese with the egg and the mint, finely chopped. Put a teaspoon of the above mixture in the middle of each round shaped pastry.

PASTRY
◇ 3 teacups flour
◇ Salt
◇ Water

Fold half of the pastry over the filling pressing the open-ends of a fork along the folded end of the pie. Fry the pies in plenty of hot olive oil over a medium fire until they are golden; place them on a platter and sprinkle with sugar. Serve these pies as an appetizer or a main dish.

Spanakotyropitákia

SPINACH AND CHEESE PIES

5-6 SERVINGS

◇ ½ kilo (1 lb 2 oz) «fyllo» pastry

◇ 1 kilo (2 lbs 4 oz) spinach

◇ 2-3 spring onions, finely sliced

◇ 2 tablespoons finely chopped dill

◇ 1 teaspoon nutmeg

◇ 350 grams (10 oz) feta cheese, crumbled

◇ 3 eggs

◇ 1 teaspoon olive oil

◇ Salt-pepper

In a pot, sauté the onions lightly in the olive oil. Shred the well washed spinach roughly, drain it well and add it to the onions; season with salt and pepper and sauté everything for another 10 minutes. Add the feta cheese, crumbled, the beaten eggs, the nutmeg, and the chopped dill and mix. Cut the «fyllo» pastry into long strips, about 5 cm (2 inches) wide. Take two strips together and brush all over the surface with olive oil; place a teaspoon of the stuffing widthwise near the one end to the strip. Fold the edge, near the filling, over it, in the shape of a cigar and then roll it down to the far end of the strip. Make sure the filling does not spill out; bake in a medium oven for about 35 minutes.

Fassólia Yígantes me Horiátika Loukánika

GIANT BEANS WITH SAUSAGES

5-6 SERVINGS

◇ 1 kilo (2 lbs, 4 oz) giant beans

◇ 2 teacups olive oil

◇ 3 medium sized onions, finely diced

◇ 1 clove garlic

◇ 3-4 ripe tomatoes

◇ 1 branch thyme

◇ 2-3 tablespoons finely chopped parsley

◇ 2 Italian or Greek style sausages

◇ Salt-pepper

Soak the giant beans in cold water overnight. The following day rinse the beans, drain through a colander and place them in a pot with water. Let them boil for about an hour. Strain the beans again and place them in a pan or a pyrex dish.

In a pot, sauté the onions in the oil. Add the finely diced tomatoes, the garlic, the thyme, the parsley, the sausages cut in thick slices, some water; season with salt and pepper and let these cook for about 10 minutes. Then pour this sauce in the pan or the pyrex dish over the beans. Bake in a medium oven for about 35 minutes.

Garídes Mikrolímano

SHRIMPS WITH TOMATOES AND FETA CHEESE

In a pot, sauté the onions in the olive oil. Add the diced tomatoes, the garlic, the bay leaf, the sugar, salt and pepper, and an adequate amount of water. Cook the sauce for about 30 minutes.

Drop the cleaned shrimps into the sauce and continue cooking for another 4 minutes. Remove from heat. Place both shrimps and sauce in a pyrex dish, spread thin slices of feta cheese over them and bake in a strong oven for 10 minutes. Serve immediately.

5 - 6 SERVINGS

- ◇ 1 kilo (2 lbs 4 oz) medium sized shrimps
- ◇ 2-3 ripe tomatoes, finely diced
- ◇ 1 teacup olive oil
- ◇ 2 onions, finely diced
- ◇ 2 cloves garlic
- ◇ 250 grams (7 oz) feta cheese
- ◇ 2 teaspoons sugar
- ◇ 1 bay leaf
- ◇ Salt-pepper

Mussels, «Island» Style ➤

Shrimps with Tomatoes
and Feta Cheese ➤

Mýdia Nissiótika

MUSSELS, «ISLAND» STYLE

5 - 6 SERVINGS

- ◇ 1 kilo (2 lbs, 4 oz) mussels
- ◇ 1 teacup olive oil
- ◇ 3 cloves garlic, sliced
- ◇ 2 tablespoons parsley, finely chopped
- ◇ 1 wineglass ouzo
- ◇ Salt and pepper

Wash mussels very well. In a pot, sauté the garlic in the olive oil. Add the mussels, the parsley and 1 wine glass ouzo (no water), salt and pepper. Cover the pot tightly and boil for 10 minutes.

Serve hot as an appetizer or a main dish.

Taramossaláta

FISH-ROE SALAD

Boil and drain the potatoes. When they are cold enough to handle, peel them and mash them. Put the mashed potatoes, the fish-roe, the grated onion in a liquidizer. Blend the ingredients for about 10 minutes adding small amounts of the refined oil and lemon juice alternately.

Serve the fish-roe salad to accompany beans, lentils and other vegetarian meals.

5 - 6 SERVINGS
- 1 kilo (2 lbs, 4 oz) peeled potatoes
- ½ teacup refined oil
- The juice of two lemons
- 1 small onion, grated

Dolmadákia Yalantzí

VEGETARIAN STUFFED VINE LEAVES

Wash the vine leaves well, scald them with boiling water and place them on a platter. Prepare the stuffing as follows: Sauté the onions in the olive oil lightly. Add the washed and strained rice, the chopped parsley and dill, the mint, a small amount of water, salt and pepper and let these cook for about 10 minutes.

Remove from heat and let the mixture cool. Place a teaspoon of the stuffing near the base of the leaf (at the stem end) and fold it as follows: press the stuffing into a small sausage – like shape and fold over it the stem end and both edges – towards the middle – inwards. Then roll the stuffed leaf over to make a tight small bundle as on p. 32. Line the bottom of a pot with vine leaves and lay the stuffed leaves in circles. When one layer is finished, begin a new one on its top.

Add some water and lemon juice and cover the last layer of stuffed leaves with an inverted plate to prevent the leaves from coming apart. Cook on medium heat for an hour and a half. Serve cold.

5 - 6 SERVINGS
- ½ kilo (1 lb, 2 oz) long-grain rice, washed and strained
- ½ kilo (1 lb, 2 oz) fresh or preserved vine leaves
- 2-3 spring (fresh) onions, finely sliced
- 2 tablespoons parsley, finely chopped
- 2 tablespoons dill, finely chopped
- 1 teaspoon mint
- 300 grams (5 oz) olive oil
- Juice of one lemon
- Salt-pepper

Htapódi Krassáto

OCTOPUS IN WINE SAUCE

◇ 1 kilo (2 lbs 4 oz) octopus

◇ 2 onions, finely diced

◇ 2-3 ripe tomatoes, roughly chopped

◇ 1-2 carrots, coarsely chopped

◇ 1 teacup olive oil

◇ 1 glass red wine

◇ Salt-pepper

In a pot, sauté the onions in the olive oil lightly. Add the octopus which has been cut into small pieces and cook for about 10 minutes stirring constantly to avoid its sticking to the pot. Pour in the wine, add the tomatoes, the carrots, salt, pepper, and an adequate amount of warm water. Cook the octopus over a medium fire for about two hours.
Serve as an appetizer.

Note: *This is not a dish recommended to those suffering stomach troubles.*

Patatossaláta

POTATO SALAD

Wrap the potatoes in aluminum foil, place them in a pan and bake them for about an hour in a medium oven. Take them out, and when they are cold enough to handle, peel them and slice them. In a bowl, mix the potatoes with the sliced onions, the chopped parsley, the olive oil. Season to taste.

5 - 6 SERVINGS

◇ 4-5 medium sized potatoes

◇ 2 small onions, sliced

◇ 2 tablespoons parsley, finely chopped

◇ ½ teacup olive oil

◇ Salt-pepper

Potato salad is served cold either as a salad or a main dish.

- *Potato Salad*

- *Fish-roe Salad*

- *Octopus in Wine Sauce*

- *Vegetarian Stuffed Vine Leaves*

Kalamarákia sto Tigáni

FRIED SQUID

Clean and wash the squid well. Season with salt and pepper. Strain the squid in a colander for a while. Flour the squid and fry them in hot oil. When they become on both sides light brown, re-

5-6 SERVINGS
- ◇ 1 kilo (2 lbs, 4 oz) squid
- ◇ 1 teacup oil for frying
- ◇ The juice of 2 lemons
- ◇ Some flour
- ◇ Salt-pepper

move them from the frying pan, place them in a serving dish and sprinkle with lemon juice. Serve warm.

Marídes sto Tigáni

FRIED WHITEBAIT (OR PICAREL)

Wash and strain the whitebait (or picarel) well through a colander. Place a good amount of flour in a cake pan adding salt and pepper. Place the whitebait in the pan and shake well so that they become well covered with flour. Fry them in boiling oil for 3-4 minutes. Take out and drain them, before you serve. They should be eaten warm with a dash of lemon juice.

3-4 SERVINGS
- ◇ 1 kilo (2 lbs 4 oz) whitebait or picarel (Maena Maena)
- ◇ 1-2 teacups oil for frying
- ◇ Some flour
- ◇ The juice of 2 lemons
- ◇ Salt-pepper

Garídes Vrastés

BOILED SHRIMPS

3 - 4 SERVINGS
- ◇ 1 kilo (2 lbs, 4 oz) shrimps
- ◇ 4 tablespoons white wine
- ◇ 1 large carrot, sliced
- ◇ 1 large onion, sliced
- ◇ 1 bay leaf
- ◇ Salt-pepper
- ◇ Mayonnaise (see p.54)

Boil the carrot, onion, bay leaf, wine in a small amount of water for about 15 minutes adding salt and pepper.
Add the shrimps and let them boil on low heat for 5-7 minutes. Remove the pot from the fire and let shrimps cool. Strain and peel them and serve them dressed with mayonnaise sauce.

Gavrokeftédes

FISH RISSOLES

Remove the heads and the entrails of the fish. Wash them well and remove their bones. Place the fish in a bowl. Add the grated onion, the mashed bread, the oregano, salt and pepper and mix everything well.
Put the mix in the blender and mince. Put the mixture in the refrigerator for two hours.
Heat the oil in a frying pan. Take spoonfuls of the fish mixture, make round shapes, coat in flour and fry them on both sides well.

4 - 5 SERVINGS
- ◇ 1 kilo (2 lbs 4 oz) small fish (such as slim anchovies)
- ◇ 2 eggs, beaten
- ◇ 5 cloves garlic
- ◇ 1 medium onion, grated
- ◇ 5 slices bread, soaked in water
- ◇ Parsley
- ◇ ½ teaspoon oregano
- ◇ Salt-pepper
- ◇ Oil for frying
- ◇ Some flour

Saganáki me Tyrí ke Avgá

FRIED CHEESE WITH EGGS

4 - 6 SERVINGS
◇ 12 eggs
◇ 4-6 portions Gruyère cheese
◇ 1 teacup flour
◇ 2 teacups olive oil

Heat the olive oil in a frying pan. Be careful not to burn or smoke. Mix 2 eggs with flour to make a paste. Divide the Gruyère cheese into portions, immerse each portion into water first, then into the egg and flour mixture, and fry it in the heated oil until it becomes on both sides light brown in colour. Fry the remaining eggs separately in olive oil and serve them alongside the fried cheese.

◄ *Fried Cheese with Eggs*

Kolokythokeftédes

PUMPKIN (SQUASH) BALLS

Slice the pumpkin (or squash), grain it and let it drain well. Put the drained pumpkin in a bowl. Add the chopped onions, the mint, salt and pepper, and mix everything well.

If the mixture is watery, add the toasted bread crumbs. Heat the oil in a frying pan. Coat spoonfuls of the pumpkin mixture in flour and fry on each side turning them once, until they become on both sides light brown.

◇ 1 large pumpkin (or squash)
◇ 1-2 onions, finely chopped
◇ Mint, finely chopped
◇ Toasted breadcrumbs
◇ Salt-pepper
◇ Some flour
◇ Oil for frying

Gardoubes

«GARDOUBES» OR OFFAL IN THE OVEN

5 - 6 SERVINGS

◇ 1 kilo (2 lbs 4 oz) green leafy vegetables (eg. lettuce, spinach beet or Swiss chards, etc.)

◇ Various herbs (e.g. dill, fennel, parsley, etc.)

◇ 2 cloves garlic

◇ 5 spring (fresh) onions

◇ Lamb' liver, lights, and intestines

◇ Olive oil

◇ Salt-pepper

Wash the lettuce, spinach beets (Swiss chards), etc. and separate their leaves. Slice the onions into medium-sized pieces and chop the herbs and the garlic finely. Cut the liver and the lights into small pieces. Turn the intestines inside out with the help of a thin stick and wash them meticulously. Take a leaf from each type of vegetable and stuff them with pieces of onion and garlic, a piece of liver and lights and various herbs. Season with salt and pepper and wrap into a small bundle. Tie the bundle up with the intestines. Place the «gardoubes» in a pan and dress them with a small amount of olive oil. Bake in a strong oven until all the ingredients are done. Serve hot.

Kokorétsi tou Fournou

BAKED «KOKORETSI»

(SAUSAGE-SHAPED OFFAL ROASTED INSIDE INTESTINES)

Turn the intestines inside out with the help of a thin stick. Wash them very carefully and then rub them with two lemons and salt, until they turn white. Cut the liver, lights, sweetbreads, etc. in small pieces. Pour the red wine all over them and season with salt, pepper and oregano.
Arrange the pieces of the offal on stainless steel skewers and in the following order: first the liver, then the lights, the sweetbreads afterwards, etc. and wrap them with the plaits of intestines. Place the «kokorétsi» in a buttered pan, sprinkle with lemon juice and bake in a medium oven.

5 - 6 SERVINGS

◇ The entrails of a medium sized lamb (such as liver, lights, sweetbreads, etc.)

◇ 2 lemons

◇ 1 water glass red wine

◇ 2 tablespoons butter

◇ The intestines of a lamb made into 5 plaits

◇ The juice of one lemon

◇ Salt-pepper-oregano

Sykotákia Ladorygani

LAMB'S LIVER IN OIL AND OREGANO

5 - 6 SERVINGS
- ◇ 1 kilo (2 lbs 4 oz) lamb's liver
- ◇ 1 teacup olive oil
- ◇ The juice of 2 lemons
- ◇ Salt-pepper-Oregano

Cut the liver into small pieces. Heat the oil in a frying pan and brown the liver pieces on strong heat. Add salt, pepper, the lemon juice and the oregano. Let them cook for about 10 minutes. Remove from fire and serve warm.

Myalá Fournou

BAKED BRAINS

5 - 6 SERVINGS
- ◇ 1 beef's brain
- ◇ 3 eggs
- ◇ 1 tablespoon butter
- ◇ Toasted breadcrumbs
- ◇ Salt-pepper

Clean the beef's brain from blood, boil it in water and purée it. Beat the eggs, add them to the mashed brain along with pepper, salt, the melted butter and mix everything well.

Butter a small pan and sprinkle with the breadcrumbs. Spread the brain mixture into the pan evenly and bake in a medium oven for half an hour. Let it cool, slice into pieces and serve.

Kremydia Yemistá

STUFFED ONIONS

5 - 6 SERVINGS
- ◇ 5-6 large onions
- ◇ ½ teaspoon red pepper
- ◇ Allspice-cinnamon
- ◇ Olive oil
- ◇ Salt-black pepper

Peel and wash the onions. With a sharp knife scoop most of their pulp out and keep the hollowed onions aside.

Heat the olive oil in a pot and sauté the onion pulp. Add the red and black pepper, the allspice, the salt and the cinnamon.

Stuff the hollowed out onions with the prepared pulp mixture and place them in a pot.

Add the appropriate amount of water and let the stuffed onions cook.

Be careful not to overcook. Serve cold.

Bakaliarópita, no 1

SALTED COD PIE, no 1

Cut the salted cod into portions and soak in water for 24 hours. Next, remove the skin and the bones and cut into very small pieces.

Heat a teacup of oil in a pot and sauté the finely diced onions in it. Add the cod pieces, the bay leaves, the salt and pepper, the nutmeg and the tomato paste diluted in a glass of water and cook for 15 minutes, stirring constantly with a wooden spoon.

Next, add the rice and cook for another minute. Remove the pot from the fire.

Prepare dough for the crust and roll it out into two sheets.

Oil a pan and lay one pastry sheet on it. Oil the crust dough and put stuffing on it. Cover the pie with the other sheet.

Pour oil over the pie and bake in a medium oven for about an hour.

◇ kilos (4 lbs 8 oz) salted or frozen cod
◇ ½ kilo rice
◇ 1 ½ teacups olive oil
◇ 2 onions, finely diced
◇ 1 tablespoon tomato paste
◇ 2 bay leaves
◇ Salt-pepper
◇ Grated nutmeg

PASTRY

◇ 1 kilo (2 lbs 4 oz) flout
◇ Salt
◇ Lukewarm water
◇ A bit olive oil

Soups

- *Lentil Soup*
- *Bean Soup*

Soupa Fakés

LENTIL SOUP

Clean the lentils and soak them overnight in water, if wanted. The following day place the lentils in a pot, cover with water and them boil over a medium fire. Allow to boil for some minutes, then drain. Put the lentils back in the pot with fresh water. Add the onions, the garlic, the tomatoes, the bay leaf, and season to taste. Let them cook on medium heat for another hour and a half. About ten minutes before removing the soup

from the fire add the vinegar and olive oil. Serve warm. Eat the lentil soup with olives or grilled herring.

5 - 6 SERVINGS
◇ ½ kilo (1 lb 2 oz) lentils
◇ 2-3 ripe tomatoes, finely chopped
◇ 2 onions, finely chopped
◇ 2-3 garlic cloves, finely chopped
◇ ¼ teacup vinegar (strong)
◇ 1 bay leaf
◇ Salt-pepper
◇ ½ teacup olive oil

Soupa Fassólia

BEAN SOUP

5 - 6 SERVINGS
◇ 2 cloves garlic
◇ ½ kilo (1 lb 2 oz) medium-sized beans
◇ 2 medium carrots, scraped and sliced
◇ 2 medium onions, finely chopped
◇ 2 ripe tomatoes, finely chopped
◇ 1 teacup olive oil
◇ Some chopped celery
◇ Salt-pepper

Soak the beans in water overnight to soften up. The following day rinse, drain and place them in a pot with water. Add the carrots, the onions, the celery, the tomatoes, the olive oil, season to taste and let everything boil over a medium fire for about 1½ to 2 hours. Serve warm. Eat the bean soup with anchovies or grilled herring and black olives.

Soupa Revythia

CHICK PEA SOUP

Soak the chick peas overnight in warm water. The following day drain the chick peas, add the baking soda, stir and rub them well.

Rinse the chick peas carefully and place them in a pot with fresh water.

Add the onions and bring the pot to the boil skimming with a slotted spoon, until the water is clear.

Cover the pot and continue cooking for 2-2 ½ hours over a low fire.

Finally, pour in the oil, season to taste and continue cooking until the chick peas are soft. Sprinkle the individual servings with lemon juice and serve.

4 - 5 SERVINGS

- ◇ ½ kilo (1 lb 2 oz) chick peas
- ◇ 1 teaspoon baking soda- Sodium Bicarbonate-optional
- ◇ 3-4 small onions
- ◇ 1 teacup olive oil
- ◇ The juice of 1 lemon
- ◇ Salt
- ◇ Pepper

Domatóssoupa me Kritharáki

TOMATO SOUP

WITH A RICE-SHAPED PASTA (ORZO)

5 - 6 SERVINGS

- ◇ ½ kilo (1 lb 2 oz) ripe tomatoes, grated
- ◇ 1 carrot, scraped and sliced
- ◇ Celery
- ◇ 6 teacups broth or fresh water
- ◇ 1 tablespoon butter
- ◇ 1 teacup «Kritharáki», a rice-shaped pasta (orzo)
- ◇ Parsley, finely chopped
- ◇ Salt-pepper

Put the broth in a pot with the tomatoes, the carrot, the celery, butter, salt and pepper and boil for 30 minutes.

Take the vegetables out of the pot and purée them. Add the pasta and the puréed vegetables to the broth and continue cooking for another 8-10 minutes on low heat.

Serve this soup garnishing the individual servings with the chopped parsley.

Kotóssoupa

CHICKEN SOUP
WITH EGG AND LEMON SAUCE

Wash the chicken well and rub it with one lemon. Place it in a pot, cover with water and let it boil for about an hour and a half on medium heat. Add the carrot, the onion, salt and pepper and continue cooking for some more minutes. When the chicken is done (test it with a fork), take it out of the pot.

Strain the broth and put it on the fire again. When the broth begins boiling, add the washed rice and continue cooking for 20 minutes.

Remove from heat.

Make the egg and lemon sauce as follows: Beat the eggs, add lemon juice to taste and beat it together. Pour in tablespoons of but not boiling brot beating at the same time. Add the egg and lemon sauce to the soup stirring constantly and rotate the pot a few times. Sprinkle the individual servings with chopped parsley and serve immediately.

5 - 6 SERVINGS
◇ 1 chicken, 1½ kilos (3 lbs 6 oz - 4 lbs 8 oz)
◇ 1 carrot
◇ 1 onion
◇ ½ teacup rice, washed and strained
◇ 3 eggs
◇ 2 lemons
◇ Parsley
◇ Salt-pepper

Country Soup ➢

Soupa Horiátiki

COUNTRY SOUP

Sauté the onions in the olive oil, until they become transparent. Add the vegetables, the bacon, the beef stock (or buillon cube) and season to taste. Let these boil on medium heat for about an hour. Serve the soup warm with dashes of lemon juice.

5 - 6 SERVINGS
◇ 2-3 medium potatoes, diced
◇ 2-3 medium carrots, scraped and diced
◇ 2-3 medium courgettes (zucchinis), diced
◇ 2-3 onions, finely chopped
◇ 2 leeks, sliced
◇ 2-3 tipe tomatoes, sliced
◇ 8 oz bacon, roughly cut
◇ 1½ teacups olive oil
◇ Beef stock or a buillon cube
◇ Some lemon juice
◇ Salt-pepper

Soupa Mayirítsa

MIDNIGHT EASTER SOUP

* Soup mainly served right after the «Resurrection Ceremony» (Midnight Mass)

Wash the lamb's liver, lights, etc. well. Turn the intestines inside out with the help of a thin stick and wash them well. Rub the intestines with salt and lemon cups, until they become white. Wash them again with plenty of water and strain them.

In a pot, cover the liver, the intestines, etc. with water and let them cook. When a foam forms in the pot, remove it with a slotted spoon.

When the offal has boiled for about an hour, remove from the broth (this broth is not to be used any more) and chop into small pieces.

Trim, wash and slice the onions and sauté them in the butter in another pot, until they wilt.

Add the pieces of offal, the dill, salt and pepper and 7-8 teacups of water to the pot and bring to the boil again for half an hour.

5 - 6 S E R V I N G S
◇ Lamb's liver, lights, intestines, etc.
◇ 3-4 spring onions
◇ 1 teacup butter
◇ ½ teacup rice, washed and strained
◇ 3-4 eggs
◇ 2 lemons
◇ The juice of 2 lemons
◇ Parsley, finely chopped
◇ Dill, finely chopped
◇ Salt-pepper

Add the rice and continue cooking for a further 20 minutes on low heat.

Remove from fire and prepare the egg and lemon sauce as described on p.50.

Add the sauce to the soup stirring constantly (keep in mind the soup should not be on the fire). Serve immediately sprinkling the soup with chopped parsley.

◁ *Trahana*

Soupa Trahaná

«TRAHANA» SOUP

5 - 6 S E R V I N G S
◇ 8 teacups beef stock o water
◇ Tomato paste (optional)
◇ 1 teacup «trahana» (see p. ;)
◇ 1 tablespoon butter
◇ Parsley
◇ Cheese, grated (optional)
◇ Salt-pepper

Dilute the tomato paste (if used) in water (or beef stock), place it in a pot and bring to the boil.

Add 1 teacup «trahana», salt and pepper and cook over a low fire for about half an hour.

Add a tablespoon of butter and serve the «trahana» soup garnished with chopped parsley. Sprinkle the individual servings with grated cheese, if wanted.

Psaróssoupa Avgolémono

FISH SOUP
WITH EGG AND LEMON SAUCE

5 - 6 SERVINGS

◇ 1½ kilos (3 lbs 6 oz) soup making large fish e.g. fresh or frozen cod, grouper, etc.

◇ 2-3 tomatoes (optional)

◇ ½ teacup olive oil

◇ 1 bay leaf

◇ ½ teacup rice, washed and strained

◇ 1 medium onion, sliced

◇ 1 carrot, sliced

◇ 2 eggs

◇ Celery

◇ The juice of 2 lemons

Clean and wash the fish. Cut it into big pieces (or leave it whole) and season it with salt. In a pot, bring 7-8 teacups of water to the boil. Drop into the boiling water the vegetables, the olive oil, the bay leaf, salt and pepper.

Cook them for about half an hour, carefully add the fish and continue cooking for a further 15 minutes. Take the fish out with a slotted spoon on to a platter. Strain the broth in case of little bones. Place the vegetables and the broth in a liquidizer and blend. Return the soup, i.e. the mashed vegetables and stock, to the heat. When it begins to boil, add the washed and strained rice and cook for about 20 minutes.

Remove the pot from the fire. Make en egg and lemon sauce («avgolémono») as follows: Beat the eggs and lemon juice. Start adding tablespoons of the soup beating at the same time. Pour the prepared egg and lemon sauce into the soup stirring slowly all the time.

Kakaviá tou Eyéou

FISH SOUP
AEGEAN STYLE

5 - 7 SERVINGS

◇ 1½ kilos (2 lbs 6 oz) various fish

◇ ½ kilo (1 lb 2 oz) onions

◇ ½ kilo (1 lb 2 oz) tomatoes

◇ Parsley

◇ 10 teacups water

◇ ½ teacup olive oil

◇ Salt-pepper

In a pot, place the water, the vegetables, salt, pepper, the olive oil and bring to the boil.

Boil for about an hour, add the fish, cover and cook for a further 10-15 minutes on low heat.

Take out the fish, strain the soup in case of little bones and serve it with the fish on a separate platter.

Sauces

- *Tomato Sauce*
- *Yoghurt Sauce with Dill*
- *Brown Sauce with Herbs*
- *Mayonnaise Sauce*

Sáltsa Mayonéza

MAYONNAISE SAUCE

n the electric mixer beat the egg yolks with the mustard, salt, pepper and the vinegar for about 5 minutes. Gradually add the oil and, when the mayonnaise begins to thicken, add the lemon juice gradually. Continue this process adding first oil then lemon juice taking care not to pour in too much oil or the mayonnaise may separate. Place the prepared mayonnaise in the refrigerator where it keeps well. Use mayonnaise to accompany fish and in various salads.

5 - 6 SERVINGS
✧ 6 egg yolks
✧ ½ litre refined oil
✧ The juice of one lemon
✧ 2 tablespoons vinegar
✧ 1 tablespoon powdere mustard
✧ Salt-pepper

Note: *If the mayonnaise separates, make a new half batch. That is, use 3 yolks, 1 tablespoon vinegar, half tablespoon mustard, salt-pepper. When this mixture begins to thicken, gradually add the separated mixture.*

Sáltsa Yaoúrti me Anitho

YOGHURT SAUCE WITH DILL

Put the yoghurt in a bowl. While mixing add the dill,

5 - 6 SERVINGS
✧ 500 grams (1 lb 2 oz) yoghurt
✧ 2 teablespoons dill, finely cut
✧ The juice of one lemon
✧ Salt-pepper

salt, pepper and the lemon juice. Serve the sauce with cucumber or lettuce salad. It also accompanies cold fish or shrimps.

Sáltsa Domáta

TOMATO SAUCE

5 - 6 SERVINGS

◇ 500 grams (1 lb 2 oz) small, ripe tomatoes, finely chopped

◇ 1 teacup olive oil

◇ 1 clove garlic

◇ 1 teaspoon basil

◇ 1 bay leaf

◇ Small amount of sugar

◇ Beef broth

◇ Salt-pepper

Place the tomatoes and olive oil in a frying pan.

Then add the salt, pepper, garlic, bay leaf, basil, sugar and some beef broth and let everything cook for about 30 minutes stirring from time to time. If the sauce is runny, add some cornflour. Serve with spaghetti, other pasta and rice.

Sáltsa Kafé me Aromatiká Hórta

BROWN SAUCE WITH HERBS

5 - 6 SERVINGS

◇ 2 teacups beef stock or a bouillon cube

◇ 1 onion, finely diced

◇ 2 carrots, finely diced

◇ 1 clove garlic

◇ 1 bay leaf

◇ 2-3 ripe tomatoes, finely diced

◇ 1 glass red wine

◇ 100 grams (3 ½ oz) bacon, finely cut

◇ 1 teacup olive oil

◇ 1 teacup flour

Pour the olive oil in a pot and sauté the onion, the carrots, the garlic and the bacon for about 10 minutes over a medium fire. Add the flour and let it turn golden. Pour in the wine and add the tomatoes, salt, pepper, the bay leaf, the beef stock and a small amount of water and cook for about an hour and a half. Taste and add more seasoning, if necessary. If the sauce is too strong, dilute it with a small amount of heavy cream.

This sauce accompanies sautéed or grilled meats well.

Sáltsa Kréma Bessamél

BÉCHAMEL SAUCE

Pour the oil in a pot. Stir in the flour and mix it well with the oil over a medium heat for 5 minutes. Add the warmed milk whisking constantly with an egg beater. Beat the eggs separately, add them to the previous mixture along with salt, pepper and nutmeg and let them cook for about 5 minutes stirring all the time.

Finally, add the grated cheese. If the sauce is too thick, add a small amount of milk. This sauce is poured over «pastitsio» and «moussaka».

5-6 SERVINGS
◇ 1 teacup flour
◇ 2 teacups milk
◇ 1 teacup refined oil
◇ 2 eggs
◇ 1 teacup kefalotyri or Parmesan cheese, grated
◇ Salt-pepper
◇ Grated nutmeg

◄ *Oil and Lemon Sauce*

◄ *Mustard Sauce*

◄ *Pepper Sauce*

◄ *Béchamel Sauce*

Sáltsa Piperáti

PEPPER SAUCE

5-6 SERVINGS
◇ 3 teacups brown sauce (see p. 55)
◇ 2 tablespoons pepper, coarsely ground
◇ 2 spoonfuls heavy cream
◇ Some red wine (optional)

Pass the brown sauce through a fine strainer and pour it into a frying pan.

Add the pepper and let it cook for about 10 minutes. Finally, add the heavy cream. Add a small amount of red wine (if needed or desired). This sauce is served to accompany sautéed meats.

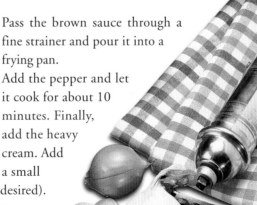

Sáltsa Kremydi

ONION SAUCE

5 - 6 SERVINGS

◇ 8 medium-sized onions

◇ 4-5 ripe tomatoes, grated

◇ 1 teacup olive or refined oil

◇ 3 slices ham

◇ Salt-pepper

◇ ½ teacup kefalotyri cheese, grated

◇ A pinch of sugar

Heat the oil in a pot and sauté the onions lightly. Add the grated tomatoes, a pinch of sugar, a small amount of water, salt and pepper and cook for 15 minutes. Finely chop the ham. Add it to the sauce and cook for another 10 minutes. Before removing the sauce from the fire sprinkle with grated cheese. It accompanies pastas or pilaf.

Sáltsa ladolémono

OIL AND LEMON SAUCE

Beat the oil along with lemon juice in a bowl. Continue by adding the parsley, salt and pepper. Serve with salads, and boiled or grilled fish.

5 - 6 SERVINGS

◇ 2 teacups olive oil refined oil

◇ The juice of one lemon

◇ 2 tablespoons parsley, finely chopped

◇ Salt-pepper

Sáltsa Moustárdas

MUSTARD SAUCE

5 - 6 SERVINGS

◇ 2 teacups mustard

◇ 2 tablespoons mayonnaise
sauce (see p. 54)

◇ 2 tablespoons vinegar

◇ 2 teacups refined oil

◇ 1 small onion, grated

◇ Salt-pepper

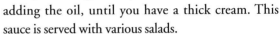

In a bowl, place the mayonnaise, the mustard, the vinegar, the grated onion, salt and pepper. With an egg beater mix them constantly while gradually adding the oil, until you have a thick cream. This sauce is served with various salads.

Sáltsa Marináti

MARINATED SAUCE

5 - 6 SERVINGS

◇ 4-5 spoonfuls flour

◇ 2 ½ glasses water

◇ 100 grams (3 ½ oz vinegar)

◇ 3 ripe tomatoes, grated

◇ Salt-pepper

◇ Rosemary

Keep any leftover oil from the frying of fish (being careful not to include any burnt sediment); pour in the flour and brown it for a few minutes.

Add the water, the vinegar, the grated tomatoes, the rosemary, salt and pepper and cook for a further 10 minutes, until the sauce thickens up. It accompanies fried fish.

Salads

- *Country (Greek) Salad, no 1*
- *White Cabbage Salad*
- *Green Beans Salad*

Saláta Horiátiki A

COUNTRY (GREEK) SALAD, no 1

Wash all the vegetables well. In a bowl, slice the tomatoes in thin quarters. Add the cucumbers (peeled and thinly sliced), the lettuce, finely cut, the onion, the oregano, the green pepper, the olives, and the caper. Dress the salad with the olive oil, salt and vinegar, and mix gently.

Finally, add the feta cheese broken into small chunks.

5-6 SERVINGS

◇ 3-4 tomatoes
◇ 2 medium-sized cucumbers
◇ 1 lettuce, finely cut
◇ 1 onion, thinly sliced
◇ 200 grams (7 oz) feta cheese
◇ 1 green pepper, thinly sliced
◇ 2-3 tablespoons vinegar
◇ 3-4 tablespoons olive oil
◇ 150 grams (5 oz) black olives
◇ 2 tablespoons caper (optional)
◇ Salt
◇ Oregano

Saláta Prássina Fassólia

GREEN BEANS SALAD

5-6 SERVINGS

◇ 1 kilo (2 lbs 4 oz) green beans
◇ 2-3 spring onions, finely sliced
◇ 2 tablespoons parsley, finely chopped
◇ 2-3 eggs, hard boiled
◇ 1 teaspoon baking soda (optional)
◇ 4-5 tablespoons olive oil
◇ 2-3 tablespoons vinegar
◇ Salt

With a sharp knife cut off the edges of the green beans. Then slice them lengthwise. Boil the beans in a pot, in salted water and soda 10 minutes over a medium fire. Remove the beans from the pot and drain them. Place them in a bowl and add the finely chopped onions, the parsley, the vinegar, the olive oil and mix. Garnish the salad with the hard boiled eggs, cut into round slices.

Vrastés Angináres Saláta

BOILED ARTICHOKE SALAD

5 – 6 SERVINGS

- ◇ 7-8 artichokes
- ◇ 2 lemons
- ◇ ½ teacup olive oil
- ◇ Salt-pepper

Peel the artichokes' outer tough leaves and cut their stalks. Slice them in the middle and remove the «hairy inside» in the middle of the heart with a sharp knife. Rub each artichoke all over with half a lemon and drop it immediately into a bowl of water. In a pot, boil water containing the juice of one lemon, salt and two tablespoons olive oil.

Drop the artichokes into the boiling water and cook for about 25-30 minutes. Drain the artichokes and serve them either with olive oil and lemon juice or with mayonnaise.

Saláta Aspro Láhano

WHITE CABBAGE SALAD

5 – 6 SERVINGS

- ◇ 1 medium-sized cabbage
- ◇ The juice of 2 lemons
- ◇ 4-5 tablespoons olive oil
- ◇ Salt

FIRST VERSION

Finely shred the cabbage with a sharp knife and place it in a bowl. Add the lemon juice, the olive oil and

SECOND VERSION

Finely shred the cabbage and place it i a bowl. Rub it with salt, for 5-10 minutes to make the cabbage juice run out. Place the cabbage in another bowl, add the lemon juice, the olive and season with salt.

Saláta me Brókola

BROCCOLI SALAD

4-5 SERVINGS

◇ 1 1/2 - 2 kilos (3 lbs 6 oz - 2 1/2 lbs) broccoli

◇ 1/2 teacup olive oil

◇ The juice of two lemons

◇ A small amount of parsley

◇ Salt

Remove the tough stems from the broccoli. Wash the broccoli and drop into boiling salted water to cook for about 20 minutes. Remove the broccoli from the fire drain through a colander. Serve the broccoli salad hot or cold with olive oil, chopped parsley and lemon juice. It accompanies fried or grilled food.

◄ *Broccoli Salad*

◄ *White Cabbage, Carrot and Olive Salad*

◄ *Field Vegetables and Courgette Salad*

Saláta Láhano, Karóta, Eliés

WHITE CABBAGE, CARROT AND OLIVE SALAD

5-6 SERVINGS

◇ 1 small white cabbage

◇ 2-3 carrots, scraped

◇ 2 hard boiled eggs

◇ 150 grams (5 oz) olives

◇ 2 tablespoons parsley, finely chopped

◇ 3-4 tablespoons olive oil

◇ The juice of two lemons

Wash, finely shred the cabbage and place it in a bowl. Add the carrots, grated, the parsley, the olives, the olive oil, the lemon juice and salt and mix. Garnish the salad with the hard boiled eggs, cut into round slices.

Saláta Kókino Láhano

RED CABBAGE SALAD

5 - 6 SERVINGS
- ◇ 1 medium-sized red cabbage
- ◇ 3-4 tablespoons vinegar
- ◇ 4-5 tablespoons olive oil
- ◇ Salt

Shred the cabbage finely with a sharp knife and place it in a bowl. Add the vinegar, the olive oil and salt and serve.

Revythossaláta me Tahíni

CHICK PEA AND «TAHÍNI» SALAD (CYPRIOT SALAD)

Immerse the chick peas into water, add the baking soda (optional) and let them stand for about 12-20 hours. Drain the chick peas and rinse them well. Place them in a pot with water and let them boil for about 2-2 ½ hours, until they become soft. Drain the chick peas through a colander and mash them. Beat the «tahíni» with a small amount of water and add it to pureed chick peas. Add the lemon juice and the olive oil stirring constantly. Mix in the garlic, mashed, salt and pepper and put the chick pea salad in the refrigerator for 2-3 hours. Serve it garnished with finely chopped parsley.

4 - 5 SERVINGS
- ◇ ½ kilo (1lb 2 oz) chick peas
- ◇ ½ teaspoon baking soda (optional)
- ◇ ½ teacup «tahíni» (see p. ;)
- ◇ The juice of 2 lemons
- ◇ ½ teacup olive oil
- ◇ 3-4 cloves garlic
- ◇ Salt-pepper

Fassólia Saláta

BEAN SALAD

5 - 6 SERVINGS

- ◇ ½ kilo (1 lb 2 oz) beans
- ◇ 2 teaspoons salt
- ◇ ½ teacup olive oil
- ◇ The juice of one lemon
- ◇ Parsley
- ◇ 1 onion, sliced
- ◇ 100 grams (3 ½ oz) black olives
- ◇ 1 ripe tomato
- ◇ Salt

Wash the beans and boil them in plenty of water for a few minutes. Remove the pot from the fire and let the beans soak for about an hour. Drain the beans through a colander, place them in the pot with warm water and bring to the boil again. Cook for another an hour and a half. Add salt and continue cooking until the beans are soft. Remove from heat and drain them again. Place the beans on a

platter with the olive oil, the parsley, chopped, the sliced onion. Dress with lemon juice and garnish with tomato slices and black olives.

Saláta Marouli

LETTUCE SALAD

5 - 6 SERVINGS

- ◇ 2-3 lettuces
- ◇ 2-3 spring onions, sliced
- ◇ 2-3 tablespoons vinegar
- ◇ 4-5 tablespoons olive oil
- ◇ 3 tablespoons dill, finely chopped
- ◇ Salt

Wash the lettuces well, cut them very finely with a sharp knife and place them in a bowl with onions and dill. Dress the salad with the olive oil, the vinegar and salt and serve.

Saláta Horiátiki B

COUNTRY (GREEK) SALAD, no. 2

5 ‑ 6 SERVINGS

- ◇ 3-4 tomatoes
- ◇ 2 medium-sized cucumbers
- ◇ 1 onion, sliced
- ◇ 150 grams (5 oz) black olives
- ◇ 2 medium-sized green peppers, finely chopped
- ◇ 2-3 tablespoons vinegar
- ◇ 3-4 tablespoons olive oil
- ◇ 200 grams (7 oz) feta cheese
- ◇ Salt - Oregano

Wash and slice the tomatoes in quarters and place them in a bowl. Add the cucumber, sliced, the onion, the peppers and the black olives.

Dress the salad with the vinegar, the olive oil, salt and oregano. Add the feta cheese, cut into chunks and serve.

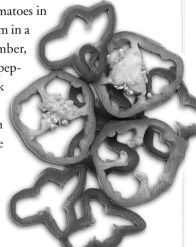

Melitzanossaláta

AUBERGINE (EGGPLANT) SALAD

Country Salad ➤
Red Cabbage Salad ➤
Tzatziki ➤
Aubergine Salad ➤

Pierce the aubergines (eggplants) with a fork, place them in a pan and bake in a medium oven for about an hour and a half.

Remove the aubergines from the oven, let them cool and prepare them as follows:

Slice each aubergine in the middle and scoop out the pulp. Finely chop the pulp, drain it to remove all liquid and place it in bowl.

Drain the diced tomatoes and add them to the aubergine pulp along with onion, salt and pepper, and parsley. Gradually add the lemon juice and oil while mixing all the time.

Note: *You may replace the refined oil with a jar of mayonnaise.*

5 ‑ 6 SERVINGS

- ◇ 3-4 tomatoes
- ◇ 4-5 aubergines (eggplants)
- ◇ 2-3 ripe tomatoes, finely diced
- ◇ 1 small onion, grated
- ◇ 2 teaspoons parsley, finely chopped
- ◇ 150 grams (5 oz) refined oil
- ◇ The juice of one lemon
- ◇ Salt-pepper

Patzária Saláta

BEET SALAD

5 - 6 SERVINGS
◇ 1 kilo (2 lbs 4 oz) beets
◇ 4-5 tablespoons vinegar
◇ 4-5 tablespoons olive oil
◇ Salt

Separate the beetroot ends from the stalks and green leaves. Wash the beetroots, scrubbing their skin. Boil them in water for about an hour and a half. Then, wash stalks and leaves and bring them to a boil for about 15 minutes. Strain both beetroots and stalks and leaves and let them cool. Peel the beetroots, cut them into slices or thick quarters and place them along with cut stalks and leaves on a platter. Season with salt. Dress with vinegar and olive oil. The best salad could accompany grilled of fried fish.

Potato Salad ➤
Beet Salad ➤
Grated Carrot and
Cucumber Salad ➤

Saláta Karóto Triméno me Agoúri

GRATED CARROT AND CUCUMBER SALAD

Scrape and grate the carrots and place them in a bowl. Wash the cucumbers, slice them finely and mix them with the grated carrots. Dress the salad with olive oil and lemon juice and season with salt.

5 - 6 SERVINGS
◇ 6-7 carrots
◇ The juice of 2 lemons
◇ 2 cucumbers
◇ 4-5 tablespoons olive oil
◇ Salt

Skordaliá

GARLIC SAUCE

5-6 SERVINGS

◇ ½ kilo (1 lb 2 oz) potatoes
◇ 4-5 cloves garlic
◇ 4-5 tablespoons olive oil
◇ 2-3 tablespoons vinegar
◇ Salt

Peel the potatoes, place them in a pot with plenty of water and let them boil over a medium fire. Drain the potatoes, purée them, season with salt and place them in a bowl.

Finely grate the garlic and mix it with the mashed potatoes. Add the oil and the vinegar and taste. Serve cold to accompany fried fish, salted cod fish, fried courgettes (zucchinis), fried aubergines (eggplants), etc.

Kounoupídi me Zabón

CAULIFLOWER WITH HAM

Cook the cauliflower in salted water. Cut it into small pieces and line a platter with it. Finely chop the ham and the parsley and spread them over the cauliflower.

Melt the butter in a pot, add the flour and let it brown lightly.

4-5 SERVINGS

◇ 1 medium-sized cauliflower
◇ 50 grams (1 ½ oz) butter
◇ ½ kilo (1 lb 2 oz) milk
◇ 1 egg yolk
◇ 2 tablespoons flour
◇ 150 grams (5 oz) ham, finely chopped
◇ Parsley
◇ Salt-pepper

Gradually pour in the milk and season with salt and pepper stirring constantly with a wooden spoon, until you have a thick sauce.

Remove the sauce from the fire; beat the egg yolk and slowly pour it into the pot.

Dress the cauliflower with this sauce.

Tzatzíki

TZATZIKI

5 - 6 SERVINGS

◇ ½ kilo (1 lb 2 oz) strained
   yoghurt

◇ 4-5 cloves garlic, finely grated

◇ 1 cucumber

◇ 4 tablespoons olive oil

◇ 2 tablespoons vinegar

◇ Salt-pepper

Grate and drain the cucumber well. Mix the yoghurt and the grated cucumber
Add the finely grated garl
Finally pour in the olive oil and vinegar alternately mixing with a mixer.
Season to taste and ser «tzatziki» as a appetizer.

Agria Hórta ke Kolokythia Saláta

FIELD VEGETABLES AND COURGETTE (ZUCCHINI) SALAD

5 - 6 SERVINGS

◇ 1 kilo (2 lbs 4 oz) field
   vegetables, e.g. dandelions

◇ ½ kilo (1 lb 2 oz) small-
   sized courgettes (zucchinis)

◇ 1 teaspoon baking soda

◇ 5-6 tablespoons olive oil

◇ The juice of 2 lemons

◇ Salt

Clean the field vegetables well and wash them many times to remove all dirt. Then drop them in boiling water and add salt and the baking soda (optional). Boil them for 10-15 minutes over a medium fire. Serve hot or cold dressed with olive oil and lemon juice.
Top and tail the courgettes (zucchinis) and prepare them in the same way.

Note: *Do not cool down the field vegetables and the courgettes by pouring cold water over them. Let them cool in their own water.*

Pies

- *Aubergine (Eggplant) Pie*
- *Artichoke Pie*
- *Field Vegetable Pies*

Anginarópita

ARTICHOKE PIE

In a pot, heat the oil and sauté the onions until transparent over a medium fire. Slice the artichoke hearts and add them to the pot along with the chopped dill. Add some water and allow them to cook for about an hour, until there is a small amount of water left in the pot. Next, place the artichoke mix in a bowl and let it cool for a while.

Beat the eggs and add them to the artichokes along with the salt and pepper, the cheese and the milk stirring constantly. Roll out the puff pastry into two pastry sheets half a centimetre thick each.

Brush a pan with olive oil or butter. Place one pastry sheet on the pan covering both its bottom and its sides. Pour the artichoke mixture over the crust and cover it with the other pastry sheet. Beat an egg yolk and spread it over the pie. Bake in a medium oven for about 45 minutes.

5 - 6 SERVINGS
- ½ kilo (1 lb, 2 oz) puff pastry
- 6 artichokes (only the hearts, without leaves)
- 4-5 spring onions, finely chopped
- 6 tablespoons dill, finely chopped
- 3 eggs
- 1 teacup milk
- 1 teacup grated Parmesan cheese
- Salt-pepper
- 1 teacup olive oil

Patatópita

POTATO PIE

5 - 6 SERVINGS
- 2 ½ kilos (5 lbs 10 oz) potatoes
- 430 grams (15 oz) olive oil
- 1 leek, finely chopped
- 1 teacup flour
- Salt-pepper
- Puff or homemade pastry

Cut the potatoes in thin slices and place them in a bowl. Add the finely chopped leek, the flour and 150 grams olive oil. Season to taste and mix everything well. Roll out the dough into 4 pastry sheets.

Line a pan with two of them and pour 70 grams (2 oz) olive oil over each one. Then, spread the potato mixture evenly and cover it with the remaining two pastry sheets pouring 70 grams olive oil on each of them. Bake the pie in a medium oven, until it turns golden brown.

Melitzanópita

AUBERGINE (EGGPLANT) PIE

5-6 SERVINGS

- ◇ 3 kilos (6 lbs, 12 oz) aubergines (eggplants)
- ◇ 4 large onions, grated
- ◇ 2 cloves garlic
- ◇ 1 teacup grated Parmesan cheese
- ◇ 1 teacup toasted breadcrumbs
- ◇ 4 eggs, beaten
- ◇ Butter
- ◇ Mint
- ◇ Some flour
- ◇ Salt-pepper

Put the aubergines in the oven for about half an hour. Then, take them out and when they are cold enough to handle, peel them. Chop their flesh, put it in a liquidizer and blend well. Sauté the grated onions in hot oil, until they look golden and add them to the mashed aubergines. Heat a part of the butter in a pot and brown the aubergine and onion mixture. Remove it from the heat and let it cool. When the mixture is cold enough, add the beaten eggs, the grated Parmesan cheese, half the breadcrumbs, the garlic cloves, the mint, season to taste and mix.

Butter and flour a pan; empty the aubergine mixture evenly, spread butter over its top, and sprinkle with the remaining breadcrumbs. Bake the pie in a medium oven.

Galatópita

MILK PIE

Pour the milk, the flour, the olive oil, the eggs, the onions, the mint, salt, pepper and the cinnamon into a pot and mix well.

Butter a pan and spread the mixture in it evenly. Bake the pie in a pre-heated oven, until it thickens.

Remove it from the oven and let it cool before cutting it into pieces. This pie is served cold.

5-6 SERVINGS

- ◇ ½ kilo (1 lb 2 oz) sheep's or goat's milk
- ◇ 2 teacups olive oil
- ◇ 2 teacups flour
- ◇ 2 onions, finely diced
- ◇ Mint
- ◇ 8-10 eggs
- ◇ Salt-pepper
- ◇ Grated cinnamon
- ◇ Butter

Píta me Piperiá

GREEN PEPPER PIE

Beat the eggs in a bowl. Add the grated feta cheese, the flour, the milk, the green peppers, salt and pepper and mix with a spatula.

Pour the mixture into a nonstick pan (or earthenware) and bake in a medium oven for about an hour.

Note: *you may add, if you wish, a crust to this pie. Bake as usual.*

3 - 4 SERVINGS
◇ 400 grams (14 oz) feta cheese, grated
◇ 1 teacups barley flour
◇ 2 teacups milk
◇ 4 green peppers, sliced
◇ Salt-pepper
◇ 3-4 eggs

Green Pepper Pie ➢

Leek Pie ➢

Prassópita

LEEK PIE

Heat the oil in a pot and sauté the leeks for about 10 minutes stirring constantly.
Beat the eggs in a bowl, add the flour, the feta cheese, the milk, the dill, the sautéed leeks, salt and pepper and mix well.

Put the mixture in a nonstick pan and bake in a medium oven for about an hour.

5 - 6 SERVINGS
◇ ½ kilo (1 lb 2 oz) leeks, chopped
◇ 4 eggs
◇ 1 teacup barley flour
◇ 2 teacups milk
◇ 250 grams (9 oz) feta cheese, crumbled
◇ ½ teacup dill, finely chopped
◇ 1 teacup olive oil

Spanakópita

SPINACH PIE

Clean and wash the spinach meticulously, then drain it well. Sauté the spring onions in the olive oil on medium heat until they become transparent but not brown. Shred the spinach in large pieces and add it to the onions. Season to taste. Cook for about 15 minutes over a medium fire so as the ingredients remain in the pot without any liquid; stir in the dill. Prepare the pastry as follows: Place the flour in a bowl, add the eggs, the melted butter, salt and as much warm water as is necessary for a bough that is pliable.

Knead the dough well and roll it out in thin pastry sheets with a rolling pin. Line an oiled pan with a pastry sheet, brush with olive oil, then lay two or three pastry sheets brushing each one with olive oil again. Spread the filling evenly and cover it with 3-4 layers of pastry sheets oiled in the same way as previously. Bake in a medium oven for about 45 minutes. Cut the spinach pie into pieces and serve it either hot or cold.

4-5 SERVINGS

- ◇ 1 kilo (1 lb, 2 oz) spinach
- ◇ 6 spring onions, finely chopped
- ◇ ½ teacup dill, finely chopped
- ◇ 1 ½ teacups olive oil
- ◇ Salt-pepper

PASTRY

- ◇ ½ kilo (1 lb, 2 oz) flour
- ◇ 2 eggs
- ◇ ½ teacup butter
- ◇ 1 teacup warm water
- ◇ Salt

Spanakópita me Kréma

SPINACH AND CREAM PIE

5 - 6 SERVINGS

◇ 1 kilo (2 lbs 4 oz) spinach

◇ Salt

FOR THE CREAM

◇ 4 eggs

◇ 1 teacup milk

◇ 250 grams (9 oz) semolina

◇ 300 grams (11 oz) feta cheese, grated

◇ 2 tablespoons butter

◇ 1 teaspoon baking powder

Clean and wash the spinach meticulously. Boil, drain it well and season with salt. Prepare the cream as follows: Beat the eggs for about 5 minutes. Then, pour in the melted butter. Dissolve the baking powder in the milk and stir it in the egg and butter mix beating everything together. Add small amounts of the grated feta cheese and the semolina alternately, beating all the time. Continue to beat for a further 10 minutes. Butter a pan; pour in a layer of the cream, about 1 centimetre (½ inch) thick. Cover the cream with half the spinach. Pour a second layer of cream over the spinach, place the remaining spinach over it, and finish with a layer of cream; spread some butter over it and bake the pie in a medium oven for an hour.

Kremydópita

ONION PIE

Chop the onions finely. Heat the olive oil in a pot and sauté the onions, until they look pale golden.

In another pot, warm the milk and gradually add the «trahana», stirring constantly, until you have a thin paste. Add the onions to the paste and season with salt and pepper. When this mixture is cold, pour in the beaten eggs.

Lay a pan with two pastry sheets brushing each sheet with olive oil. Pour the mixture into the pan evenly, cover it with the remaining pastry sheets (both brushed with olive oil) and bake in a medium oven for about 45 minutes.

5 - 6 SERVINGS

◇ 1 kilo (2 lb 4 oz) milk

◇ 2-3 onions

◇ 1 teacup sweet «trahana»

◇ 8 eggs, beaten

◇ Salt and pepper

◇ Olive oil

◇ 4 puff pastry sheets

Pítes me Agrióhorta

FIELD VEGETABLE PIES

5 – 6 SERVINGS

◇ 1 kilo (2 lbs 4 oz) field
   vegetables, e.g. dandelions

◇ 2 onions, finely diced

◇ 250 grams (9 oz) feta cheese

◇ 1 teacup corn meal

◇ 2 teacups milk

◇ 3 eggs

◇ Salt-pepper

PASTRY

◇ ½ kilo (1 lb 2 oz) flour

◇ 2 eggs

◇ ½ teacup butter

◇ 1 teacup warm water

◇ Salt

Heat the oil in a pot and sauté the onions lightly. Add the corn meal stirring with a spatula. Next, pour in the milk stirring constantly to prevent the mixture from becoming lumpy.

Remove the pot from the fire and add the cheese and the eggs.

Wash the vegetables very well. Scald them in boiling water for 2-3 minutes. Drain them and add them to the pot with the other ingredients stirring constantly.

Prepare the pastry as follows:

Put the flour in a bowl. Beat the eggs and add them to the flour along with the melted butter, salt and as much warm water as is necessary to make a dough that is pliable.

Knead the dough well and with a rolling pin roll

out thin, round pastry leaves. In the centre of each leaf put a spoonful of the stuffing. Spread egg yolk around the edges of the crusts and fold half of the pastry over the filling forming crescent shaped pies. Be careful not to let the filling seep out.

Put the prepared pies in a buttered pan and bake for about 35 minutes in a medium oven.

◄ *Spinach Pie*

◄ *Field Vegetable Pies*

Myzithropitákia

CHEESE PIES «MYZITHRA»

Crumble the cheese in a bowl. Beat the eggs and pour them over the crumbled cheese. Add the chopped dill and mix well with a spatula.

Prepare the pastry; roll it out into pastry sheets and cut in triangle shapes. Put a tablespoon of the cheese mixture in the middle of each triangle; fold and stick the edges firmly to make sure the filling does not spill out. Place the pies in a buttered pan. Beat the egg yolk with some water and polish each pie with it. Bake in a medium oven for about 45 minutes.

5 - 6 SERVINGS

◇ ½ kilo (1 lb, 2 oz) «Myzithra» cheese (see p. 213) or ½ kilo cottage cheese together with ¼ kilo feta cheese

◇ 3 eggs

◇ 2 tablespoons dill, finely choped

◇ An egg yolk for brushing the pies

PASTRY

◇ ½ kilo (1 lb 2 oz) flour

◇ 2 eggs

◇ ½ teacup butter

◇ 1 teacup warm water

Píta apó ta Yánena

PIE, IOANENA STYLE

5 - 6 SERVINGS

◇ 700 grams (1 lb 9 oz) Gruyère cheese

◇ 250 grams (9 oz) butter

◇ 3 eggs

◇ 500 grams (1 lb 2 oz) milk

PASTRY

◇ 3 teacups flour

◇ 1 teacup yoghurt

◇ 5 tablespoons butter

◇ Salt

◇ Water (if needed)

Prepare the pastry (adding a teacup yoghurt) and roll out the dough into four pastry leaves («fylla»). Butter a pan, lay one pastry leaf onto it, brush it with butter and sprinkle grated Gruyère cheese all over its surface. Lay a second leaf, sprinkle it with cheese again and then a third one exactly the same way as the preceding ones, brushing each sheet with melted butter. Finally lay the fourth sheet of pastry, brush it with butter and with the help of a sharp knife make incisions on this top layer.

In a bowl, beat the eggs, stir in the milk and pour over the pie. Bake it in a medium oven, until it looks golden brown.

Tyrópita

CHEESE PIE, No 2

5 - 6   S E R V I N G S

- ◇ 1 kilo (2 lb, 4 oz) milk
- ◇ 8-10 eggs, beaten
- ◇ 1 kilo (2 lb, 4 oz) feta cheese
- ◇ 250 grams (9 oz) kefalotyri cheese, grated
- ◇ 250 grams (9 oz) butter
- ◇ Pinch of dill
- ◇ ½ kilo (1 lb, 2 oz) «fyllo» pastry
- ◇ 250 grams (9 oz) fine semolina

Pour the milk and the semolina in a pot and cook over a low fire, stirring constantly, until you have a thick cream. Add the butter, the beaten eggs, salt and pepper. Finally, add the grated kefalotyri and feta cheese, the finely chopped dill and mix well. Put layers of ½ the «fyllo» pastry in a pan brushing each one with melted butter. Make sure that the edges of the pan are lined with the pastry so that they can be folded over the filling later. Spread the filling evenly, fold any overlapping edges over it and add the remaining «fyllo» pastry on top, brushing each pastry sheet with butter. Cut the top layers of the pastry in square shapes with a knife and bake the cheese pie in a medium oven, until its top is golden brown.

Tyrópita horís Fyllo

CHEESE PIE
(WITHOUT «FYLLO» PASTRY), NO 1

Beat the eggs in a bowl, add the melted butter and the yoghurt and mix. Add the feta and Gruyère cheese, cut in small pieces. Finally, add the baking soda (or baking powder) and the flour gradually, while stirring all the time. Pour the cheese mixture into a buttered pan. Bake the pie in a medium oven for about 25 minutes.

This pie is served either hot or cold.

5 - 6   S E R V I N G S

- ◇ 400 grams (14 oz) feta cheese
- ◇ 100 grams (3 ½ oz) Gryyère cheese
- ◇ 3 eggs
- ◇ 250 grams (9 oz) yoghurt
- ◇ 1 teacup flour
- ◇ ½ teaspoon baking soda (or baking powder)
- ◇ 200 grams (7 oz) butter

- *Aubergine Pie*
- *Small Cheese Pies*
- *Spinach and Cheese Pies*

Píta me Eliés

OLIVE PIE

Remove the olive pits and chop the olives finely. Add the mint and the finely diced onion. Place the flour, the baking powder and the olive oil in a bowl and mix. Add the warm water and continue mixing, until you have a fluid dough.

Add the olive mixture to the dough and continue to mix. Flour a pan and pour the mixture into it. Bake in medium oven for about an hour.

5-6 SERVINGS

◇ 3 ½ teacups flour
◇ 1 teacup black olives
◇ 2 teacups warm water
◇ Dried and ground mint
◇ 1 small onion, finely diced
◇ 2 teaspoons baking powder
◇ 1 glass olive oil

Makaronópita

MACARONI PIE

Boil the macaroni in plenty of salted water. Drain through a colander and place in a bowl. Add the grated kefalotyri and feta cheeses, the eggs (beaten), the milk, a small amount of olive oil and mix.

Butter a pan and line it with 2 pastry sheets brushing each one with melted butter. Spread the macaroni mixture evenly and cover it with the other two pastry sheets, buttered in the same way. Bake at 250oC, until the pie is golden brown.

5-6 SERVINGS

◇ ½ kilo (1 lb 2 oz) thick macaroni
◇ 1 kilo (2 lbs 4 oz) feta cheese
◇ 10 eggs
◇ 150 grams (5.5 oz) kefalotyri cheese
◇ 750 grams (1 lb 11 oz) milk
◇ Olive oil-butter
◇ 4 puff pastry sheets

Píta me Kymá

MINCED MEAT PIE

5 - 6 SERVINGS

◇ 1 ½ kilos (3 lbs 6 oz) minced lamb

◇ 1 kilo (2 lbs 4 oz) onions

◇ 5 tablespoons butter

◇ 10 eggs, lightly beaten

◇ 1 teacup milk

◇ 2 teacups semolina

◇ Salt-pepper

◇ Cinnamon

◇ 1 kilo (2 lbs 4 oz) «fyllo» pastry

Heat half the butter in a and sauté one finely diced onion. Add the minced lamb, salt and pepper, the cinnamon, two teacups water an cook, until all the wa gone. Quarter the remaining onions and boil them in broth (or in water containing the bones of the lamb) in another pot. When the onions are done, take them out and purée them. Strain the broth and keep only two teacups of it.

Prepare a cream with the milk, the semolina and the broth. When this cream is cold enough, add the puréed onions, the beaten eggs, the remaining butter, the cinnamon, salt and pepper.

Brush the bottom and sides of a pan with butter and line it with half the sheets of «fyllo» pastry, brushing each one with melted butter. Spread the minced meat evenly and pour the cream mixture over it.

Cover with the remaining sheets of «fyllo» pastry, brushing each one with butter, particularly the top one. Bake the pie in a medium oven, until its top starts to turn pale golden.

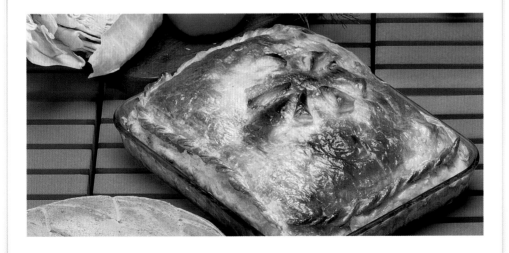

Kolokythópita, no 1

COURGETTE (ZUCCHINI) PIE, no 1

Top and tail the courgettes (zucchinis). Next, wash, grate them and season with salt and pepper. Add the grated feta cheese, the melted butter, the eggs and mix. Prepare the pastry as described on previous pages and roll out a pastry sheet.

Line a buttered pan with the pastry sheet and spread the courgette mixture evenly.

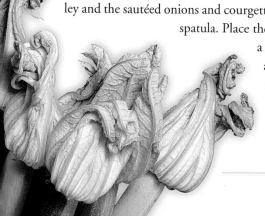

Bake in a medium oven for about 25 minutes, until the top of the pie is golden. Before removing the pie from the oven bore holes into it with a fork to help liquid evaporate. Let the pie cool, cut it into pieces and serve.

5 - 6 SERVINGS

◇ 4-5 large courgettes (zucchinis)

◇ 5-6 eggs, lightly beaten

◇ 500 grams (1 lb 2 oz) feta cheese, grated

◇ 3 tablespoons butter

◇ Salt-pepper

◇ A home-made pastry

Courgette Pie, no 2 ➤
Cheese Pies «Myzithra» ➤
Courgette Pie, no 1 ➤
Ham Pies ➤

Kolokythópita, no 2

COURGETTE (ZUCCHINI) PIE, no 2

Heat the olive oil in a pot and lightly sauté the onions. Add the sliced courgettes (zucchinis) and sauté for another 10 minutes.

Beat the eggs in a bowl, add the feta cheese, the parsley and the sautéed onions and courgettes; mix with a spatula. Place the mixture into a non-stick pan and bake in a medium oven for about an hour.

5 - 6 SERVINGS

◇ 1 kilo (2 lbs 4 oz) medium-sized courgettes sliced

◇ 400 grams (14 oz) feta cheese, cut in chunks

◇ 6 eggs

◇ 3 spring onions, finely chopped

◇ ½ teacup parsley, finely chopped

◇ 1 teacup olive oil

Zabonópita

HAM PIES

In a pot, sauté the onions lightly in the olive oil. Add the chopped ham, the sliced red peppers and the parsley. Sauté for a further 10 minutes stirring with a spatula. Sprinkle the flour into the pot and let it cook for a while longer. Stir in the milk and remove the pot from heat.

In a bowl, beat the eggs lightly and pour them into the pot. Finally add the feta cheese stirring constantly.

Roll out the puff pastry and cut it in round shapes with a pastry cutter. Place a tablespoon of the ham mixture in the middle of each round shaped pastry, brush the edges of the pastry with a beaten egg yolk and cover it with another round shaped pastry. Press the edges of the pie with the help of the open-ends of a fork to make sure the filling does not seep out.

Oil a pan lightly and place the small pies in lines. Beat an egg yolk with some water and polish each pie with it. Bake the ham pies in a medium oven for about 30-35 minutes.

5 - 6 SERVINGS
◇ 300 grams (11 oz) ham, chopped
◇ 2 red peppers, sliced
◇ 2-3 spring onions, finely chopped
◇ 250 grams (9 oz) feta cheese
◇ ½ teacup flour
◇ 2 teacups milk
◇ 1 teacup olive oil
◇ 3 eggs
◇ 2 tablespoons parsley, finely chopped
◇ 2 eggs yolks
◇ 500 grams (1 lb, 2 oz) puff pastry

Bakaliarópita, no 2

SALTED COD PIE

5 - 6 SERVINGS

- ◇ 1 ½ kilos (3 lbs, 6 oz) salted or frozen cod fish
- ◇ 500 grams (1 lb, 2 oz) rice
- ◇ 1 ½ teacups olive oil
- ◇ 3 eggs
- ◇ 1 large onion, finely diced
- ◇ 4 cloves garlic, chopped
- ◇ Parsley-mint
- ◇ Salt-pepper
- ◇ 2 teaspoons tomato paste
- ◇ 2 glasses water

PASTRY
- ◇ ½ kilo (1 lb, 2 oz) flour
- ◇ Olive oil
- ◇ Salt
- ◇ Warm water

Cut the cod into pieces and soak it overnight in plenty of water (this course is followed in case you are using salted cod fish).

The following day, boil the cod, remove its bones, cut it into small pieces and place them in a bowl. Add the rice, the finely diced onion, the garlic, the parsley, the mint, the olive oil, the tomato paste, the eggs, salt and pepper and the 2 glasses of water. Mix all ingredients well.

Prepare the pastry as follows:

Place the flour in a bowl, add some olive oil, salt and as much warm water as is necessary for a dough that is pliable. Knead the dough well by hand and roll it out into 2 pastry sheets.

Brush a pan with olive oil. Line the pan with one sheet. Spread the filling over it. Cover with the other sheet and sprinkle with water. Bake in a medium oven.

Ryzópita

RICE PIE

5 - 6 SERVINGS

- ◇ ½ kilo (1 lb 2 oz) rice
- ◇ 10 eggs
- ◇ 2 teacups water
- ◇ Olive oil
- ◇ Salt
- ◇ 10-12 pastry sheets
- ◇ ½ kilo (1 lb 2 oz) feta cheese, cut in chunks

Half cook the rice, drain it and rinse it with cold water. Place the rice in a bowl. Add the butter, the eggs, the cheese, season with salt and mix.

Lay 3 sheets of «fyllo» pastry in a pan oiling each one separately. Lay the remaining pastry sheets with rice filling between each one except for the last two sheets which should have only olive oil spread between them. Cut the top layers of «fyllo» pastry into pieces and bake the pie in a strong oven, until its top looks golden brown.

Eggs

- *Fried Eggs with Spinach*
- *Scrambled Eggs with Tomatoes and Green Peppers*
- *Fried Eggs in Potatoes*
- *Sausage and Green Pepper Omelettes*

Avgá Mátia me Spanáki

FRIED EGGS WITH SPINACH

Clean and wash the spinach and shred it roughly. In a pot, sauté the onions in one teacup oil. Add the spinach, the dill, the nutmeg, a small amount of water, season to taste, and let them cook for about 15 minutes on medium heat. Remove the spinach from the fire and prepare each serving portion as follows: In a small pyrex pan, spread two tablespoons of the spinach mixture, break 2 or 3 eggs over it and bake in a medium oven for 5 minutes. Continue this process, until all the eggs are cooked. Serve hot.

4 SERVINGS

◇ 12 eggs

◇ 500 grams (1 lb 2 oz) spinach

◇ 2-3 spring onions, finely sliced

◇ 300 grams (11 oz) refined oil

◇ 2 tablespoons dill

◇ 1 teaspoon nutmeg

◇ Salt, pepper

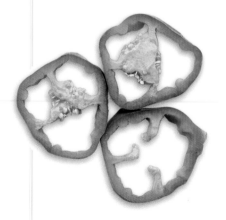

Omeléta me Loukánika ke Prássini Piperiá

SAUSAGE AND GREEN PEPPER OMELETTES

In a frying pan, sauté the sausages and the green peppers in two tablespoons oil for about 5 minutes over a medium fire.

Prepare each omelette as follows:

Beat 3 eggs in a bowl adding two tablespoons of the sausage and green mixture. Season with salt and pepper. Heat two tablespoons oil over a medium fire in another frying pan. Pour in the egg mixture and fry the omelette on one side. Flip it over with a spatula and let it cook on the other side.

Continue this process with the remaining ingredients, until all the omelettes are prepared. Serve hot.

4 SERVINGS

◇ 12 eggs

◇ 400 grams (14 oz) Italian or Greek style sausages, sliced

◇ 3-4 green peppers, sliced

◇ 300 grams (11 oz) refined oil

◇ Salt-pepper

Avgá «Fylakisména» se Patátes

FRIED EGGS IN POTATOES

4 SERVINGS

- ◇ 8 eggs
- ◇ 8 medium sized potatoes
- ◇ 200 grams (7 oz) or 1 teacup butter
- ◇ Salt-pepper

Wash and wrap the potatoes in aluminum foil. Place them in a small pan and bake in a medium oven for about an hour and a half. Remove the baked potatoes from the oven, unwrap them and when they are cold enough to handle, cut off their tops. Scoop about half of the potatoes pulp out.

Season the potatoes with salt and pepper. Place one tablespoon butter on every hollowed out potato and then break an egg into each one. Return the stuffed potatoes to the oven and cook for a further 5 minutes. Serve hot.

Avgá «Darména» i Kayaná

SCRAMBLED EGGS
WITH TOMATOES AND GREEN PEPPERS

In a frying pan, place the tomatoes, the sugar, the green peppers, 3 tablespoons olive oil, salt and pepper and let them cook for about 10 minutes. Remove the tomato sauce from heat and prepare each serving portion as follows:

In another frying pan, heat two tablespoons olive oil on a medium fire. Beat 3 eggs in a bowl, add 2 tablespoons of the prepared tomato sauce, 2 tablespoons milk, salt and pepper to taste, mix and empty this mixture in the heated oil stirring from time to time with a spatula. Cook the «Kayaná» until the eggs are done but not too solid.

Repeat this process, until all the ingredients are used. Serve hot.

Note: *«Kayaná» might also be placed on slices of black toasted bread.*

4 SERVINGS

- ◇ 12 eggs
- ◇ 3-4 ripe tomatoes, finely diced
- ◇ 203 green peppers, thinly sliced
- ◇ Olive oil
- ◇ ½ teacup milk
- ◇ 2 teaspoons sugar
- ◇ Salt-pepper

Avgá se Domátes

FRIED EGGS IN TOMATOES

Wash the tomatoes and cut a thin round slice off the top stem end of each one. Scoop the tomato pulp out and keep the tomatoes aside. Shred the pulp finely, place it in a frying pan with the oil, the parsley, the sugar, salt and pepper and let them cook for 10 minutes. Then, half fill the hollowed out tomatoes with this sauce; place the stuffed tomatoes in a pan and bake in a medium oven for about 15 minutes.

Take the tomatoes out.

Break an egg into each one and bake again for a further 10 minutes. Serve hot.

4 SERVINGS
◇ 8 eggs
◇ 8 medium-sized, ripe tomatoes
◇ ½ teacup olive or refined oil
◇ 2 teaspoons sugar
◇ 2 teaspoons parley, finely chopped
◇ Salt-pepper

Courgette and Red Pepper Omelettes ➤
Fried Eggs in Tomatoes ➤
Mushroom and Parsley Omelettes ➤

Omeléta me Manitária ke Maintanó

MUSHROOM AND PARSLEY OMELETTES

In a frying pan, heat two tablespoons oil, add the mushrooms and parsley and sauté for about 5 minutes over a medium fire.

Then beat 3 eggs in a bowl, add 2 tablespoons of the mushroom and parsley mix and season with salt and pepper.

In another frying pan, heat 2 tablespoons oil. Add the egg mixture, some sausage slices and some more parsley. Stir a little and let the omelette fry on both sides. Repeat this process with the remaining eggs, sausages, parsley and mushroom mixture. Serve the omelettes hot.

4 SERVINGS
◇ 12 eggs
◇ 400 grams (14 oz) mushrooms, sliced
◇ 400 grams (14 oz) sausages, sliced, e.g. frankfurters
◇ 4 tablespoons parsley, finely chopped
◇ 300 grams (11 oz) refined oil
◇ Salt-pepper

Oméléta me Kolokythia ke Kókini Piperiá

COURGETTE (ZUCCHINI) AND RED PEPPER OMELETTES

Heat 2 tablespoons oil in a frying pan and sauté the courgettes (zucchinis) and the red peppers for 10 minutes over a medium fire. Beat 3 eggs in a bowl, add 2 tablespoons of the courgettes (zucchini) and pepper mix and season with salt and pepper. In another frying pan, heat 2 tablespoons of oil, add the egg-courgette mixture, stir and let the omelette fry on one side. With a spatula flip it over and let it fry on the other side too. Prepare all the omelettes by repeating this process. Serve hot.

4 SERVINGS
- 12 eggs
- 3-4 medium-sized courgettes (zucchinis), cut in round slices
- 3-4 red peppers, thinly sliced
- 300 grams (11 oz) refined oil
- Salt-pepper

Oméléta me Spanáki

SPINACH OMELETTE

Clean and wash the spinach well. Place it in a pot without water and let it cook in its own moisture for about 10 minutes. Drain the spinach and cut it up. Finely slice the onions, chop the dill and sauté both ingredients in a frying pan containing half the butter. Add the spinach, the salt and the pepper. Cook everything for a few minutes and empty in a bowl. Beat the eggs adding the milk and the crumbs. Heat the remaining butter in a frying pan and pour in the egg mix and the spinach.

Fry the omelette on both sides (approximately 10 minutes for each side). Serve hot, cut in wedges.

4 SERVINGS
- 8 eggs
- 1 kilo (2 lbs 4 oz) spinach
- 1 teacup butter
- 3-4 spring onions
- 1 teacup milk
- 1/2 teacup toasted breadcrumbs
- A bit of dill
- Salt-pepper

Avgá me Myalá Keftédes

EGG AND BRAIN RISSOLES

4 SERVINGS

◇ 5 eggs

◇ 1 beef brain

◇ 1 teacup toasted breadcrumbs

◇ Salt-pepper

◇ A little parsley

◇ Oil for frying

Clean the brain trying to get its outer membrane off. Crush with a mortar and pestle to form a paste. Slowly add the eggs and continue beating so that the mix will keep together. Season to taste. Gradually add the crumbs until you have a paste that is neither too thick nor too runny.

Heat the oil in a frying pan. (It must be very hot). Drop spoonfuls of the mixture into the oil and let the rissoles fry on both sides. Serve hot garnished with chopped parsley.

Omeléta me Bámies

OMELETTE WITH OKRA
(LADIES' FINGERS)

Cut off the okra (ladies' fingers) stems and wash them. Then, chop the okra in small pieces. Heat the oil in a frying pan and cook the okra for about 10 minutes over a low fire. Next, pour in the grated tomatoes, some water, salt and pepper.

5-6 SERVINGS

◇ 6 eggs

◇ 1 teacup olive oil refined oil (not completely filled)

◇ 1 tablespoon butter

◇ ½ kilo (1 lb 2 oz) tomatoes

◇ ¼ kilo (9 oz) okra (ladies' fingers)

◇ Salt-pepper

Cover the frying pan and let the okra simmer, until all the water is gone and only the oil is left. Add the butter and remove the pan from heat. Beat the eggs and stir in the frying pan. Fry the omelette on both sides over a low fire. Serve hot.

Avgá Mátia me Kremydia

FRIED EGGS WITH ONIONS

4 SERVINGS

◇ 12 eggs

◇ 2-3 onions, sliced

◇ 300 grams (11 oz) olive or refined oil

◇ Salt-pepper

◁ *Fried Eggs with Aubergines*

◁ *Fried Eggs with Onions*

◁ *Fried Eggs with Minced Meat*

Sauté the onions lightly in a frying pan with half a teacup oil for 10 minutes. In a pan, spread the onions evenly and break the eggs over them. Season with salt and pepper and bake in a medium oven for 5 minutes. Serve hot, as soon as they are taken out of the oven.

Omeléta me Kymá

MINCED MEAT OMELETTE

Brown slightly the onion and the minced meat in a frying pan. When all its water evaporates, add the butter and stir with a wooden spatula. When the onion looks golden brown, add the tomato, the milk, a small amount of water, salt and pepper and simmer until all the water is gone.

In the meantime, cook the liver separately, chop it finely and add it to the cooked minced meat. In another frying pan, heat the oil (it must be very hot). Beat the eggs and mix them with the grated cheese. Season with salt and pepper and drop them in the heated oil; let the omelette fry on one side. Before flipping it over, place the meat-liver mixture on it, and make a roll; lower the fire, turn the omelette over and let it fry on the other side. Serve the omelette hot.

4 SERVINGS

◇ 3 eggs

◇ 1 tablespoon butter

◇ 3 tablespoons minced meat, cooked

◇ 1 tablespoon liver, finely chopped

◇ 2 tablespoons milk

◇ 1 tomato, finely diced

◇ 1 onion, grated

◇ 1 tablespoon grated cheese

◇ Salt-pepper

◇ Oil for frying

Avgá Mátia me Melitzánes

FRIED EGGS WITH AUBERGINES

Cut the aubergines (eggplants) in two, lengthwise. With a sharp knife cut square shapes in the aubergine pulps. Fry the aubergine halves over a medium fire for 10 minutes and then place them in a pan. With a spoon scoop about half of the pulp out from each one. Place the pulp along with some oil in a frying pan. Add the tomatoes, the onions, the parsley, the sugar, salt and pepper and cook for about 10 minutes. Fill each aubergine with this mixture.
Be careful not to over-fill them as there should be left enough room for the eggs.
Bake the stuffed halves for about 15 minutes in a medium oven. Remove the aubergines from the oven and break one or two eggs over each aubergine. Return the pan to the oven for another 5 minutes. Serve hot.

4 SERVINGS
- ✧ 4 medium-sized aubergines (eggplants)
- ✧ 2 teaspoons parsley, finely chopped
- ✧ 2 onions, finely diced
- ✧ 2 fresh, ripe tomatoes, finely diced
- ✧ 600 grams (1 lb 5 oz) refined oil
- ✧ 2 spoonfuls sugar
- ✧ Salt-pepper

Omeléta me Ryzi

RICE OMELETTE

Wash and slice the tomatoes, season with salt, sprinkle the sugar all over and fry them in the oil (or butter). Boil the rice as for pilaf and drain it. Beat the eggs and pour them into the rice. Add salt, pepper, milk, the grated cheese and stir. Lightly sauté the onion in the oil (or butter) in a frying pan. Pour the egg mixture into the frying pan and flatten its surface. Fry the omelette on both sides. Serve it hot garnished with the fried tomato slices.

4 SERVINGS
- ✧ 8 eggs
- ✧ 5 tomatoes
- ✧ 100 grams (3 1/2 oz) rice
- ✧ 1 onion, finely diced
- ✧ 4 tablespoons grated cheese
- ✧ 2 tablespoons milk
- ✧ Salt-pepper
- ✧ A pinch of sugar
- ✧ Oil for frying (or butter)

Avgokeftédes me Sáltsa

EGGBALLS WITH SAUCE

5-6 SERVINGS

◇ 10 eggs

◇ 5 slices of bread, soaked in water

◇ A little parsley, finely chopped

◇ Mint

◇ Salt-pepper

◇ ½ kilo (1 lb 2 oz) ripe tomatoes

◇ Oil for frying

◇ 2 spoonfuls olive oil

Squeeze excess moisture from the soaked bread. Place it in a bowl. Beat the eggs, add them to the bread together with the mint, the parsley, 2 spoonfuls olive oil, salt and pepper. Mix together all the ingredients by hand to form a consistent mixture. Heat plenty of oil in a frying pan. When the oil is very hot, drop spoonfuls of the mix in the frying pan.

In the meantime, grate the tomatoes. When the «eggballs» are done, remove them from the oil. Pout the grated tomatoes in the oil, season with salt and let them boil. When the sauce is done, drop the «eggballs» and cook a little while longer. Serve the «eggballs» in the tomato sauce.

Avgá Mátia me Kymá

FRIED EGGS WITH MINCED MEAT

4 SERVINGS

◇ 12 eggs

◇ 500 grams (1 lb 2 oz) minced meat

◇ 1 onion, finely diced

◇ 1-2 ripe tomatoes, finely diced

◇ 1 clove garlic

◇ ½ teacup olive or refined oil

◇ 1 cinnamon stick

◇ 1 bay leaf

◇ 1 teaspoon oregano

◇ Salt-pepper

In a pot, heat ½ a cup of oil and sauté the onion. Add the minced meat, the tomatoes, the oregano, the garlic, the cinnamon, the bay leaf, salt and pepper, and a small amount of water and let everything cook on medium heat for about 30 minutes until all the water is gone.

If you wish, place two tablespoons of meat on a toasted slice of bread in a pyrex dish and break 2 or 3 eggs over this. Otherwise, simply spread the minced meat in the pyrex dish and break the eggs over it.

Bake in a medium oven for 5 minutes.

Avgá Mátia me Anginátes

FRIED EGGS WITH ARTICHOKES

Prepare the artichokes as follows: peel their tough outer leaves, cut their stalks and with a spoon remove the furry insides. Rub the artichokes with a cup of lemon and place them in a bowl containing water and the juice of one lemon (to prevent the artichokes turning black). Let the artichokes stand for about an hour. Proceed to boil the artichokes in salted water with lemon juice for about 35-40 minutes over a medium fire and keeping the lid on the pot.

4 SERVINGS
◇ 8 eggs
◇ 8 medium-sized artichokes
◇ 200 grams (7 oz) butter or margarine
◇ 2 lemons
◇ Salt-pepper

Line the artichokes in a pyrex dish. Fill the centre of every artichoke by breaking an egg into it. Also add a teaspoon of butter, salt and pepper to each one. Bake in a medium oven for 5 minutes. Serve hot.

Peasant Omelettes ➤
Fried Eggs with Sliced Tomatoes ➤
Fried Eggs with Artichokes ➤

Avgá Mátia me Fétes Domátas

FRIED EGGS WITH SLICED TOMATOES

After cutting the tomatoes in thick slices arrange them in four individual-sized pyrex dishes. Season with salt and pepper and sprinkle with sugar.

Pour two tablespoons oil into each pyrex dish and bake them in a strong oven for 10-15 minutes.

Remove the dishes from the oven and break 2 or 3 eggs in each dish. Return the dishes to the oven and continue to bake in a slightly less than medium oven for 5 minutes. Serve hot.

4 SERVINGS
◇ 12 eggs
◇ 2-3 ripe tomatoes
◇ 1 teacup refined oil
◇ 2 teaspoons sugar
◇ Salt-pepper

Omeléta Horiátiki

PEASANT OMELETTES

In a frying pan, heat 3-4 tablespoons oil and sauté the onions for 5 minutes. Remove the olive pits and cut the olives in half. Add the olives to the onions along with the red peppers and the feta cheese and continue cooking for another 5 minutes.

Beat 3 eggs in a bowl and add two tablespoons of the «onion-cheese-olive-pepper» mixture.

In another frying pan, heat 2 tablespoons oil over a medium fire and pour in the omelette mixture. Fry the omelette on both sides. Repeat this process until all the omelettes are prepared. Serve hot.

4 SERVINGS

- ◇ 12 eggs
- ◇ 200 grams (7 oz) feta cheese, cut in chunks
- ◇ 100 grams (3 ½ oz) black olives
- ◇ 2 red peppers, sliced
- ◇ 2 onions, cut in round slices
- ◇ 500 grams (1 lb 2 oz) refined oil
- ◇ Salt-pepper

Avgá me Fréska Fassolákia

OMELETTE WITH GREEN BEANS

Clean and wash the green beans and cut off their edges with a sharp knife. Boil them in a pot with water. When the beans are done, take them out of the pot and drain them. Sauté the onions in a frying pan with butter, add the green beans, the parsley, finely chopped, salt and pepper, and brown everything for about 5 minutes. Beat the eggs and pour them over the contents of the frying pan. Fry the omelette on both sides. Serve hot.

4 SERVINGS

- ◇ 1 kilo (2 lbs 4 oz) green beans
- ◇ 1 teacup butter
- ◇ 8 eggs
- ◇ 3-4 onions, finely diced
- ◇ Parsley
- ◇ Salt-pepper

Avgá Mátia me Rígani ke Elies

FRIED EGGS WITH OREGANO AND OLIVES

5 - 6 SERVINGS

◇ 6 eggs

◇ ½ kilo (1 lb 2 oz) tomatoes, peeled & sliced

◇ 200 grams (7 oz) salami

◇ 4 tablespoons oregano

◇ 10 black olives

◇ 200 grams (7 oz) kasseri or cheddar cheese

◇ 1 teacup olive or refined oil

◇ Salt-pepper

Heat the oil in a frying pan. Add the salami, cut into pieces and remove it from the frying pan, once it is half cooked. Peel the tomatoes. Slice them and put them into the frying pan for a few minutes. Having sliced the cheese, break the eggs, one by one, over the tomato slices. Place the salami, the cheese and the olives (washed and halved) between the eggs. Sprinkle with oregano, salt and pepper. Serve hot.

Omeléta me Garídes

OMELETTE WITH SHRIMPS

Wash the shrimps and boil them in salted water. Remove their heads, peel their bodies and slice them. Sauté the shrimps in half the butter in a pot. Beat the eggs, add the parsley, finely chopped, salt and pepper and mix well.

5 - 6 SERVINGS

◇ 5 eggs

◇ 250 grams (9 oz) shrimps

◇ A little parsley

◇ 100 grams (3 oz) butter

◇ Salt-pepper

Heat the remaining butter in a frying pan and pour in the egg mixture. Stir in the shrimps and fry the omelette on both sides over a low fire. Serve hot.

Pasta Rice

- «*Grandmother's*» *Spaghetti*
- *Macaroni and Meat Pie*
- *Spaghetti with Cream*

Pastítsio

MACARONI AND MEAT PIE

5 - 6 SERVINGS

◇ 1 kilo (2 lbs 4 oz) macaroni No 3 (thick)

◇ ½ kilo (1 lb 2 oz) minced meat

◇ 2 medium-sized onions, finely diced

◇ 2-3 ripe tomatoes, finely diced

◇ 2 teacups olive oil

◇ 1 bay leaf

◇ Pinch of basil

◇ 150 grams (5 oz) kefalotyri or Parmesan cheese, grated

◇ Salt-pepper

Sauté the onions in a teacup of oil, until they turn golden. Add the minced meat and sauté it with the onions stirring constantly, until all the lumps of the meat are dissolved. Add the tomatoes, salt and pepper, the bay leaf, the basil and some water.

Let everything cook over a medium fire for about 30 minutes.

Half cook the macaroni in plenty of salted water, cool them down and drain. In a frying pan, heat the second cup of oil and pour it over the macaroni. In the meantime, prepare the béchamel sauce as follows:

Lay out a layer of macaroni in a pyrex dish or pan, sprinkle it with cheese and cover with the minced meat mix, you have prepared. Spread the remaining macaroni over the minced meat layer, sprinkle again with cheese and cover with the béchamel sauce. Sprinkle the sauce with grated cheese. Bake the «pastitsio» in a strong oven for 20 minutes. Take it out of the oven, let it cool down, cut it into square pieces and serve immediately.

❧ BÉCHAMEL SAUCE ❧

Pour the oil in a pot. Stir in the flour and mix it well with the oil over a medium heat for 5 minutes. Add the warmed milk whisking constantly with an egg beater. Beat the eggs separately, add them to the previous mixture along with salt, pepper and nutmeg and let them cook for about 5 minutes stirring all the time. Finally, add the grated cheese.
If the sauce is too thick, add a small amount of milk.

BÉCHAMEL SAUCE

◇ 1 teacup flour

◇ 1 teacup refined oil

◇ 4 teacups milk

◇ 3 eggs, beaten

◇ 150 grams (5 oz) kefalotyri or Parmesan cheese, grated

◇ Salt-pepper

◇ Pinch of nutmeg

Makarónia me Kréma (Xynókrema)

SPAGHETTI WITH CREAM (OR SOUR CREAM)

4 SERVINGS

◇ ½ kilo (1 lb 2 oz) medium sized spaghetti

◇ 150 grams (6 oz) black olives

◇ 200 grams (7 oz) ham, sliced

◇ 200 grams (7 oz) parmesan cheese, grated

◇ 150 grams (6 oz) butter

◇ 150 grams (6 oz) heavy cream (Crème Fraîche)

◇ Salt

Boil plenty of salted water in a pot. Add the spaghetti. Be careful not to overcook them. When they are done, cool them down with much fresh water and drain.

Melt the butter in a pot over a medium fire. Add the ham and the olives and sauté for 5 minutes (approximately).

Drop the spaghetti and stir with a wooden spoon. Then, add the grated cheese and the cream which has been lightly beaten. Serve hot.

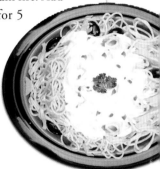

Makarónia tis Yayás

«GRANDMOTHER'S» SPAGHETTI,
WITH PEPPER AND MUSHROOM SAUCE

5-6 SERVINGS

◇ ½ kilo (1 lb 2 oz) medium-sized spaghetti

◇ 2-3 green peppers

◇ 2-3 red peppers

◇ 2 onions, sliced

◇ 200 grams (7 oz) mushrooms, sliced

◇ 2 teacups olive oil

◇ 2 teacups cheese, grated (Kefalotyri or Parmesan)

◇ Salt-pepper

Lightly sauté the onions in a teacup olive oil over a medium fire. Add the peppers, thinly sliced, the mushrooms, 2 teacups water, the salt and pepper. Cook for about 20 minutes. Boil the spaghetti in plenty of salted water, be careful not to overcook them. When they are done, cool them down in fresh water and drain. In another pot, heat the second teacup of olive oil, drop the spaghetti and sauté for 5 minutes. Pour in the pepper and mushroom sauce while stirring. Serve hot with grated cheese.

Hylopítes Metsóvou

NOODLES, METSOVO STYLE

5-6 SERVINGS

◇ ½ kilo (1 lb 2 oz) noodles («hylopites»)

◇ 4-5 ripe tomatoes, finely diced

◇ 250 grams (9 oz) lard or bacon

◇ 2 onions, finely chopped

◇ 2 cloves garlic

◇ 100 grams (3 ½ oz) olive oil

◇ Salt-pepper

◇ Grated Kefalotyri or Parmesan cheese

Cut the lard or bacon into big pieces and place them in a pot with the olive oil. Add the onions and the garlic cloves and sauté for ten minutes over a medium fire.

Continue by adding the tomatoes the salt and pepper, some water or beef broth (if it is preferred). Add the noodles (1 part noodles to 3 parts liquid) and cook over a medium fire for about 25 minutes. Serve hot as a main dish. Sprinkle over with the grated cheese.

Noodles, Metsovo Style ➤

Pasta (Orzo) Casserole ➤

Youvétsi Kritharáki

PASTA (ORZO) CASSEROLE

4-5 SERVINGS

◇ ½ kilo (1 lb 2 oz) «kritharaki», a rice-shaped pasta (orzo)

◇ 1 onion, finely diced

◇ 3 ripe tomatoes, finely diced

◇ 1 large, green pepper

◇ 2 cloves garlic

◇ 1 teacup olive oil

◇ 1 large tin of ham

◇ Some celery, chopped

◇ Salt-pepper

◇ Feta cheese, crumbled

Heat the oil in a pot and sauté the onion lightly. Add the tomatoes, the celery, the green pepper, the cloves of garlic (all finely chopped), salt and pepper and sauté for a further 5 minutes.

In the meantime, empty the contents of the pot into a casserole dish (earthenware or pan), add some warm water and the pasta. Season with salt and pepper, stir and bake in a pre-heated oven at a medium temperature for about an hour.

Five minutes before removing the pan from the oven, add the ham which has been cut into small pieces. Mix the ham with the pasta and leave it in the oven to create a crust (the oven should be turned off).

Serve hot, sprinkled with feta or any other type of cheese.

Kritharáki Smyrnáyko

PASTA (ORZO), SMYRNA STYLE

Lightly sauté the onions and the garlic cloves in the oil on medium heat.

Add the tomatoes, salt and pepper, a pinch of sugar and cook for another 10 minutes.

Pour in 1 ½ kilos (3 lbs 6 oz) warm water or beef broth and bring to boil again.

Add the pasta and cook over a medium fire for approximately 25 minutes.

Serve hot with grated cheese.

5 - 6 SERVINGS
- ½ kilo (1 lb 2 oz) «kritharaki», a rice-shaped pasta) orzo
- 3-4 ripe tomatoes, finely diced
- 2-3 onions, finely diced
- 2-3 cloves garlic
- 1 ½ teacups kefalotyri or Parmesan cheese, grated
- 1 ½ teacups olive oil
- Pinch of sugar
- Salt-pepper

Makarónia me Melitzánes

SPAGHETTI WITH AUBERGINES
(EGGPLANTS)

5 - 6 SERVINGS
- ½ kilo (1 lb 2 oz) medium sized spaghetti
- 1 kilo (2 lbs 4 oz) aubergines (the slim variety) (eggplants)
- ½ kilo (1 lb 2 oz) grated tomatoes
- ½ teacup olive oil
- 2 tablespoons butter
- Salt-pepper
- 1 teacup kefalotyri or parmesan cheese, grated

Cut the stalks and bottom ends of the aubergines (eggplants), slice them in the middle and make incisions down their centre. Salt the aubergines and let them stand in water for an hour.

Place the tomatoes, the oil, and some water in a pot, season with salt and pepper and boil for 5 minutes. Drain the aubergines and put them in the pot with the other ingredients. Add some more water, lower the heat and continue cooking for another 30-40 minutes.

In another pot, boil the spaghetti in plenty of salted water, strain and place on a platter; heat the butter until boiling, pour over the spaghetti and sprinkle with grated cheese. Place the aubergines over the spaghetti pouring the sauce from the pot on top.

Makarónia me Saligária

SPAGHETTI WITH SNAILS

3 - 4 SERVINGS

◇ 1 kilo (2 lbs 4 oz) snails
◇ 3 medium-sized onions
◇ 4-5 ripe tomatoes, grated
◇ 1 ½ teacups olive oil
◇ 300 grams (12 oz) spaghetti
◇ Salt-pepper

Clean the snails carefully, and drop them into boiling water for 25-30 minutes.

Heat the oil in a pot and sauté the onions; add the grated tomatoes, salt and pepper, and let them cook.

Next, remove the back part of the snails, wash them very well and drop them into the pot with the sauce. Stir. Add 3 glasses of water and boil for about 15 minutes.

Add the spaghetti which has been already half cooked in another pot with plenty of salted water.

Pastítsio me Prássa

MACARONI WITH LEEKS IN THE OVEN

Boil the macaroni in a pot with plenty of salted water (be careful not to overcook). Drain in a colander. Heat half the butter until boiling and pour it over the macaroni; empty the contents of the pot into a buttered pan.

Top and tail the leeks. Discard the coarse outer leaves, particularly at the green end, rinse them and cut them lengthwise, in strips 10 cm (4 inches) long. Boil them in salted water, then strain them and sauté them in a pot with the remaining butter for 10 minutes. Cover the macaroni with the leeks and stick the hot pepper in one corner of the pan. Bake in a medium oven for 40 minutes. In the meantime, bring a pot with water to the boil; with the boiling water scald the olives and spread them all over the contents of the pan. About 10 minutes before baking is over, pour the beaten eggs over the «pastitsio», season with salt and pepper and return it to the oven, until the crust, that has been created, turns golden brown. Serve this dish either hot or cold.

4 - 5 SERVINGS

◇ ½ kilo (1 lb 2 oz) macaroni
◇ 1 ½ kilos (3 lbs 6 oz) leeks
◇ 100 grams (3,5 oz) butter
◇ 1 ½ kilos (3 lbs 6 oz) ripe tomatoes
◇ 1 pepper (hot)
◇ 100 grams (3,5 oz) black olives
◇ 3 eggs
◇ Salt-pepper

Ryzi tou Psará

RICE WITH SHRIMPS AND MUSSELS

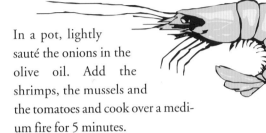

5 - 6 SERVINGS

- ◇ ½ kilo (1 lb 2 oz) rice
- ◇ 250 grams (9 oz) shrimps
- ◇ 250 grams (9 oz) mussels
- ◇ 2-3 ripe tomatoes, finely diced
- ◇ 2 onions, sliced
- ◇ 2 teacups olive oil
- ◇ 2 tablespoons ouzo
- ◇ Salt-pepper

In a pot, lightly sauté the onions in the olive oil. Add the shrimps, the mussels and the tomatoes and cook over a medium fire for 5 minutes.

Pour in the ouzo. Add the rice, as much water as is necessary (i.e. one part rice, two parts water), season with salt and pepper and continue cooking for another 15 minutes. Serve hot.

◅ *Rice with Shrimps and Mussels*

◅ *Spinach Rice*

Spanakóryzo

SPINACH RICE

5 - 6 SERVINGS

- ◇ 1 kilo (2 lbs 4 oz) spinach
- ◇ 1 ½ teacups long grain rice, washed and strained
- ◇ 3-4 spring onions coarsely cut
- ◇ ½ teacup dill, finely chopped
- ◇ 2 teacups olive oil
- ◇ 2 lemons

In a pot, sauté the onions in the oil. Wash the spinach well, shred it roughly and add it to the pot with the onions.

Cook over a medium fire for 5 minutes.

Add the rice, 2 teacups water, the dill, salt and pepper and continue cooking for another 15 minutes. Serve the spinach rice either hot or cold with dashes of lemon juice.

Piláfi me Angináres

PILAF WITH ARTICHOKES

Remove the tough outer leaves of the artichokes. With a sharp knife scoop all the «hairy inside» in the middle of the heart out. Cut their stems and use them only if they are tender.

Rub the artichokes with a lemon and immerse them immediately into cold water.

Boil the artichokes in plenty of water to which the juice of 2 lemons has been added. When they are done, remove them from the water.

Filter the water in which the artichokes were boiled

6   S E R V I N G S
◇ 12 artichokes
◇ 1 ½ teacup butter
◇ 1 onion
◇ 3 teacups rice
◇ 2-3 lemon
◇ Dill, finely chopped
◇ Salt-pepper

and cook the rice in it (2 parts water to 1 part rice) for 15-20 minutes over a low fire. Stir the rice and place the artichokes over it with their back parts facing upwards. Season with salt and pepper. Heat some butter in a frying pan, lightly sauté the onion in it and pour over the rice and the artichokes. Serve hot, sprinkled with dill.

Krokétes me Ryzi

CROQUETTES WITH RICE

Boil the rice for about 15 minutes in salted water stirring with a wooden spoon.

Take off the heat, sprinkle with the grated cheese, mix and let it stand for 5 minutes. Then, add the pine nuts, the ham (finely chopped), the raisins, salt and pepper; stir well to make a mixture. In a bowl, beat the remaining 2 eggs. Take spoonsfuls of the above mix and shape them as you like.

Dip the croquettes into the beaten eggs, roll them in the breadcrumbs and fry them in hot oil, until they become golden brown. Serve them either hot or cold.

5 - 6   S E R V I N G S
◇ ½ kilo (1 lb 2 oz) rice
◇ 4 eggs
◇ 4-5 slices ham
◇ 1 teacup grated cheese
◇ 3-4 tablespoons grated pine nuts
◇ 50-60 grams (2 oz) white raisins
◇ Parsley
◇ Mint   ◇ Salt-pepper
◇ 1 teacup toasted breadcrumbs

Ryzi me Araká ke Manitária

RICE WITH GREEN PEAS AND MUSHROOMS

4-5 SERVINGS

◇ ½ kilo (1 lb 2 oz) long-grain rice

◇ ½ teacup mashed tomato

◇ 200 grams (7 oz) butter

◇ ½ kilo (1 lb 2 oz) mushrooms, sliced

◇ 1 kilo (2 lbs 4 oz) green peas

◇ 1 teacup cheese, grated

◇ Salt-pepper

Clean and wash the rice and place it in a pot with boiling water. Let the rice cook for about 15 minutes, then pour in cold water and strain it. Heat a tablespoon butter in a frying pan and pour over the drained rice which, in the meantime, has been returned to the pot.

Prepare the tomato sauce as follows:

Heat a spoonful of butter in another pot; add the mashed tomatoes, season with salt and cook for 5 minutes.

Shell the peas (in case that fresh peas are used), wash them and  boil them in salted water. When all the water is gone, drop a spoonful of butter and let them sauté.

Wash the mushrooms well, strain them and separately sauté them in butter as well.

Serve as follows:

Place the rice on a platter with the peas on one end and the mushrooms on the other. Sprinkle the rice with the grated cheese and pour the tomato sauce on top.

Skordóryzo

GARLIC RICE

3-4 SERVINGS

◇ ½ kilo rice (1 lb 2 oz)

◇ 10 grams (36 oz) garlic

◇ 1 teacup olive oil

◇ Salt-pepper

Boil some water in a pot. Add the garlic, finely diced, and let it simmer for about 10 minutes; then, pour in the olive oil.

Add the rice, washed and strained, salt and pepper and continue cooking, until the rice has absorbed all the water (10-15 minutes). Serve hot.

Skordomakárona

GARLIC MACARONI

In a pot, pour 1 teacup oil and 1 teacup water, add the tomatoes, the garlic, salt and pepper and the sugar and boil for about 20 minutes.

Boil the macaroni in plenty of salted water. Cool them down in cold water and drain.

Heat the second teacup of oil in another pot, add the macaroni and sauté them stirring all the time. Pour the prepared sauce on top, sprinkle with grated cheese and serve this dish hot as a first course.

5 - 6 SERVINGS
- ½ (1 lb 2 oz) macaroni (No 3)
- 3-4 ripe tomatoes, finely diced
- 4-5 cloves garlic, finely diced
- 2 teacups Kefalotyri or Parmesan cheese, grated
- 2 teacups olive oil
- 2 teaspoons sugar
- Salt-pepper

Garlic Macaroni ➤

Octopus with Short, Thick Macaroni ➤

Htapódi me Koftó Makaronáki

OCTOPUS WITH SHORT, THICK MACARONI (TUBETTI)

5 - 6 SERVINGS
- ½ kilo (1 lb 2 oz) short, thick macaroni (tubetti)
- 1 kilo (2 lbs 4 oz) octopus
- 2 medium-sized onions, finely diced
- 3-4 ripe tomatoes, finely diced
- 1 bay leaf
- 2 teacups olive oil
- Salt-pepper

Pour the oil into a pot and sauté the onions lightly. Wash the octopus, cut it into small pieces and add it to the pot with the onions while stirring.

Add the tomatoes, the bay leaf, salt and pepper and

cook for about an hour over a medium fire.

Then, add the macaroni and continue cooking for about 25 minutes. Add some more water, if needed. Serve this dish hot as a first course.

Lazánia sto Fourno

LASAGNA IN THE OVEN

Squeeze excess moisture from the soaked bread. Place it in a bowl with the minced meat, the raw egg, salt and pepper, half the grated cheese and mix well by hand making sure that the bread is incorporated. Heat half the oil in a frying pan. Make small round shapes, the size of olives and fry them.

Add the remaining oil to the frying pan and sauté the onion in it. Pour in the tomatoes, add the salt and pepper and cook for half an hour.

Boil the lasagna in plenty of salted water and drain them in a colander. Butter a pan, pour in a part of the tomato sauce, then place a layer of lasagna over the sauce and pour some more sauce over the pasta. Sprinkle with cheese. Place half the meat balls, half the sausages (sliced) and half the boiled eggs (also sliced) over the layers of pasta and sauce. Cover with another layer of lasagna and continue with the remaining ingredients as before. Sprinkle the final layer with cheese and spread pieces of butter over the surface.

Bake in medium oven for 20 minutes. Serve hot.

5 - 6 SERVINGS

- ◇ ½ kilo (1 lb 2 oz) lasagna
- ◇ 1 kilo (2 lbs 4 oz) ripe tomatoes, finely diced
- ◇ 1 onion, finely diced
- ◇ 250 grams (9 oz) minced meat
- ◇ 1 raw egg
- ◇ 4 boiled eggs
- ◇ 1 slice bread, soaked in water
- ◇ ½ kilo (1 lb 2 oz) grated kefalotyri cheese
- ◇ 1 teacup olive oil
- ◇ 250 grams (9 oz) Italian or Greek style sausages
- ◇ Salt-pepper

Koftó Makaronáki me Yaourti ke Tyrí

SHORT, THICK MACARONI WITH
YOGHURT AND CHEESE

Boil the macaroni in salted water and drain in a colander. Dilute the yoghurt in a small amount of hot water and add it to the macaroni.

In a frying pan, heat the butter, sauté the onion in it and pour it over the macaroni.

Serve hot with grated cheese.

4 - 5 SERVINGS

- ◇ ½ kilo (1 lb 2 oz) short, thick macaroni (tubetti)
- ◇ ½ kilo (1 lb 2 oz) strained yoghurt
- ◇ 3 - 4 tablespoons butter
- ◇ 1 onion, finely diced
- ◇ Salt - ◇ Grated cheese

Hylopítes me Pikántiki Sáltsa

NOODLES IN A SPICY SAUCE

Boil salted water in a pot, drop the noodles and cook them for about 15 minutes. Drain the noodles and cool them down with cold water.

Prepare the sauce as follows:
Heat half the butter in a pot and sauté the finely chopped carrots in it. Add the ham, (finely chopped) and sauté with the carrots. Pour in the tomatoes, add the celery (without chopping it), salt and pepper and the necessary amount of water and cook, until the sauce thickens.

Place the noodles on a platter, heat the remaining butter and pour it over them.

Pour the sauce over the noodles (having previously removed the celery). Sprinkle with grated cheese. Serve hot.

3 - 4 SERVINGS
◇ ½ kilo (1 lb 2 oz) noodles (hylopites)
◇ 3-4 ripe tomatoes, finely diced
◇ 4 tablespoons butter
◇ 3-4 carrots, finely chopped
◇ 3-4 slices ham
◇ Celery (small amount)
◇ 1 teacup grated cheese
◇ Salt-pepper

Bakaliáros me Koftó Makaronáki

SALTED CODFISH WITH SHORT, THICK MACARONI (TUBETTI)

Cut the cod into portions and soak in a bowl with water overnight changing the water frequently during the evening and the next morning, to remove the salt (in case you are using salted cod). On the following day heat the oil in a pot and sauté the onion lightly. Add the grated tomatoes, salt and pepper the macaroni, the necessary amount of water and bring the pot to the boil. When the macaroni is half done, add the pieces of cod (strained) without stirring. Rotate the pot to avoid sticking. Cook for a further 10-15 minutes and take off the fire. Let the macaroni absorb more of the liquid. Serve hot.

5 - 6 SERVINGS
◇ 1 kilo (2 lbs 4 oz) salted cod (it can be replaced by fresh or frozen cod)
◇ 1 teacup olive oil
◇ 3 ripe tomatoes, grated
◇ 1 large onion, grated
◇ 500 grams (1 lb 2 oz) short, thick macaroni (tubetti)
◇ Salt-pepper

Meats

- *Beef with Okra (Ladies' Fingers)*

- *Beef with Black-eyed Beans*

- *Rolled Beef with Stuffed Onions*

- *Beef with Courgettes (Zucchinis)*

Moscharáki me Kolokythia

BEEF WITH COURGETTES (ZUCCHINIS)

Cut the meat into small pieces (two per serving). Heat the oil in a pot and sauté the onions, until they are golden. Continue by adding the meat. Sauté it, constantly stirring, until it looks golden brown.

Next, add the tomatoes, salt, pepper, the mint and an amount of water. Let everything boil for about 2 hours.

Meanwhile top and tail and rinse the courgettes (zucchinis). Slice them in the middle and fry them lightly. Twenty minutes before the meat finishes cooking, place them in the pot. Continue cooking over a low fire. Serve hot.

5-6 SERVINGS

◇ 6 servings (1 ½ kilos or 3 lbs 6 oz) beef
◇ 1 kilo small courgettes (zucchinis) (2 lbs 4 oz)
◇ 2-3 ripe tomatoes, finely diced
◇ 2 onions, finely diced
◇ 1 teacup olive oil
◇ 1 spoonful ground mint
◇ Salt-pepper

Roló me Kremydia Yemistá

ROLLED BEEF WITH STUFFED ONIONS

5-6 SERVINGS

◇ 1 ½ kilos (3 lbs 6 oz) beef
◇ 2 onions, coarsely cut
◇ 2 ripe tomatoes, finely diced
◇ 1-2 carrots
◇ 1 clove garlic
◇ 1 glass red wine
◇ 1 teacup olive oil
◇ Salt-pepper

Tie the meat with white string, heat the oil in a pot and sauté it, until it becomes golden brown on all sides. Pour in the wine. Add the onions, the tomatoes, the carrots, the garlic, salt and pepper and an amount of water and let them boil for about two and a half hours, keeping the pot covered. Remove the meat from the pot and place it on a platter. Take the vegetables out, purée them and return them to the pot. Continue cooking for a while. Add some more wine, if it is desired.

Finally, slice the meat, pour the vegetable sauce over it and garnish it with stuffed onions (see p.39) covered with béchamel sauce.

Moscharáki me Bámies

BEEF WITH OKRA (LADIES' FINGERS)

6 SERVINGS

◇ 6 servings (1 ½ kilos or 3 lbs 6 oz) beef

◇ 1 kilo okra (2 lbs 4 oz)

◇ 2-3 ripe tomatoes, finely diced

◇ 2 onions, finely diced

◇ 2 tablespoons parsley, finely chopped

◇ 1 teacup olive oil

◇ 1 teacup vinegar

◇ Salt-pepper

Wash and strain the beef and cut it into small pieces. Heat the oil in a pot and sauté the onions lightly. Add the meat and while stirring it allow it to become golden brown.

Then, add the tomatoes, salt, pepper, the parsley and an amount of water. Allow everything to boil for about two hours.

In the meantime, prepare the okra by cutting off their stems with a sharp knife. Place them in a bowl with salt and vinegar and let them stand for about an hour. Drain them and half an hour before the meat finishes cooking, place them in one side of the pot. Continue cooking over a low fire.

Serve hot.

Moscharáki me Fassólia Mavromátika

BEEF WITH BLACK-EYED BEANS

Cut the beef into small pieces (two pieces to each serving). Heat the oil in a pot and sauté the onions lightly. Add the meat. Sauté it while constantly stirring, until it becomes golden. Next, add the tomatoes, the garlic, salt and pepper and an amount of water and let everything boil for about an hour over a medium fire. Wash the black-eyed beans, and place them on one side of the pot. Continue boiling for another hour and a half. Serve hot.

6 SERVINGS

◇ 6 servings (1 ½ kilos or 3 lbs 6 oz) beef

◇ 1 teacup olive oil

◇ 1 kilo (2 lbs 4 oz) black-eyed beans, soaked in water overnight to make cooking them easier

◇ 2-3 ripe tomatoes, finely diced

◇ 2 onions, finely diced

◇ 1 clove garlic

◇ Salt-pepper

Hirinó me Láhano

PORK WITH CABBAGE

4 - 6 SERVINGS

◇ 6 servings (about 1-1 ½ kilos or 2 lbs 4 oz - 3 lbs 6 oz) pork

◇ 1 ½ kilos cabbage (3 lbs 6 oz)

◇ 2-3 ripe tomatoes, finely diced

◇ 3 onions, finely diced

◇ 1 teacup olive oil

◇ Salt-pepper

Wash the meat, strain and cut it into serving portions. Sauté the onions over a medium fire. Add the meat pieces and allow them to brown for about 5-10 minutes. Then, add the tomatoes, salt, pepper and some water and let them boil for approximately an hour and a half. In the meantime, prepare the cabbage by cleaning it and cutting it into large pieces. Place it on one side of the pot and let everything boil for another 30 minutes. Serve hot.

Pork with Cabbage ➤

Pork Chops in Wine ➤

Brizóla Hiriní Krassáti

PORK CHOPS IN WINE

6 SERVINGS

◇ 6 pork chops

◇ 1 glass red wine

◇ 500 grams (1 lb 2 oz) small, round potatoes

◇ 500 grams (1 lb 2 oz) green beans

◇ 500 grams (1 lb 2 oz) carrots

◇ ½ teacup butter

◇ Salt-pepper

◇ Oregano

◇ Oil for frying

Wash and strain the pork chops. Sprinkle them with salt, pepper and oregano. Heat the oil in a frying pan. Fry the pork chops over a medium heat 10 minutes on each side. Add the wine to the pork chops and prepare the vegetables as follows:

Cut off the edges of the green beans and peel the carrots. Then cut both the carrots and the beans in small sticks and wash them well. Boil them in water, drain them and sauté them in butter seasoning to taste. Peel the potatoes and either fry them or bake them in the oven. Garnish the pork chops with the vegetables and potatoes and serve them warm as a second course.

Arnáki exochikó

COUNTRY LAMB

6 SERVINGS

- ◇ 6 servings leg of lamb (1 ½ kilo approx.) (3 lbs 6 oz)
- ◇ 4-5 fresh onions (spring onions)
- ◇ 500 grams round potatoes (1 lb 2 oz)
- ◇ 300 grams peas (11 oz)
- ◇ 300 grams unsalted cheese (11 oz)
- ◇ 2 tablespoons dill, finely chopped
- ◇ Salt-pepper
- ◇ ½ kilo fyllo pastry (1 lb 2 oz)
- ◇ 1 ½ teacups oil
- ◇ 1 teacup butter, melted

Heat the oil in a pot and sauté the onions in it. Add the boned lamb and brown for about 10 minutes. Adding a small amount of water allow the meat to boil for approximately one hour. Then add the vegetables and let everything boil for another 20 minutes. Remove the pot from the fire.

Next, cut the fyllo pastry into strips of about 20 cm. width and at the end of each strip place a piece of lamb and some of the vegetables. To the lamp and vegetable mix add pieces of cheese. With a brush, spread butter on the ends of the filo. Wrap each piece carefully as you would with dolmadakia.

Finally, place the «parcels» in a buttered pan and bake in a medium oven for about 35-40 minutes.

Serve hot. (see photo p. 134-135)

Arnáki me makarónia hodrá

LAMB AND MACARONI

Heat the oil in a pot and sauté the onions. Cut the meat into small pieces (2 pieces = 1 serving). Place it in the pot along with the onions and sauté all for 5-10 minutes, stirring constantly. Next add the red wine, the tomatoes, the garlic and the salt and pepper. Cook over a low fire for approximately 2 hours.

Boil the macaroni (not too much), and serve them alongside the lamb. Pour sauce from the pot over the macaroni and sprinkle with grated cheese.

5-6 SERVINGS

- ◇ 6 servings lamb (1 ½ kilo approx.) (3 lbs 6 oz)
- ◇ 1 kilo macaroni (no 3) (2 lbs 4 oz)
- ◇ 2-3 ripe tomatoes, diced
- ◇ 1 teacup oil
- ◇ 1 glass red wine
- ◇ 1 clove garlic
- ◇ 1 teacup grated cheese
- ◇ Salt, pepper

Arní me Strangistó Yaoúrti

LAMB WITH STRAINED YOGHURT SAUCE

Wash the lamb well and put it in a pan. Add salt, butter and water and place the pan in a medium oven. Let it bake well.

Prepare the yoghurt sauce as follows:

In a bowl, beat the yoghurt with salt and pepper slightly. Beat the egg whites separately (do not make them stiff). Then, add the yolks. Beat both a little while longer and add the beaten eggs to the yoghurt beating all the time. Take the pan out of the oven; remove the lamb from the pan and pour the yoghurt sauce in the pan. Return the pan to the oven and bake, until the sauce thickens up.

Place the lamb back in the pan with the sauce and bake again. When the contents of the pan are golden brown, remove it from the oven and serve.

5 - 6 SERVINGS

- ⟡ 2 kilos (4 lbs 8 oz) lamb
- ⟡ 4-5 eggs
- ⟡ 1 large teacup butter
- ⟡ 1 large teacup water
- ⟡ 1 ½ kilos (3 lbs 6 oz) strained yoghurt
- ⟡ Salt-pepper

Arnáki Anixiátiko Lemonáto

LAMB WITH LEMON SAUCE

5 - 6 SERVINGS

- ⟡ 6 servings lamb (1 ½ kilos approx. or 3 lbs 6 oz)
- ⟡ 1 kilo potatoes (2 lbs 4 oz), peeled and sliced
- ⟡ 2-3 carrots
- ⟡ 3-4 spring onions, finely diced
- ⟡ 2 tablespoons dill, finely chopped
- ⟡ The juice of one lemon
- ⟡ 1 teacup olive oil
- ⟡ Salt-pepper

Wash and strain the lamb. Heat the oil in a pot and sauté the onions over a medium fire.

Add the meat, cut into serving portions and seasoned with salt and pepper, and an amount of water.

Let the lamb cook for about an hour and a half. Then, add the carrots, peeled and sliced lengthwise, the potatoes, the dill and the lemon juice. Continue cooking over a low fire for another 45 minutes. Serve hot.

- Stewed Lamb with Potatoes

- Country lamb

- Lamb and macaroni

- Lamb with Lemon Sauce

Arní Yahní me Patátes

STEWED LAMB WITH POTATOES

Heat the oil in a pot and sauté the onions. Wash and strain the lamb and cut it into servings. Add the meat to the sautéed onions and let it brown for about 5-10 minutes, stirring all the time. Add the tomatoes, the salt and the pepper and a small amount of water and let everything boil for about an hour and a half over a medium fire. Finally, peel the potatoes and cut them into round or oblong pieces; partially fry them and add them to the lamb. Continue cooking for a further 30 minutes. Serve hot.

6 SERVINGS

- 6 servings (1 ½ kilos approximately or 3 lbs 6 oz) lamb
- 1 kilo (2 lbs 4 oz) potatoes
- 2-3 ripe tomatoes, finely diced
- 2 onions, finely diced
- Olive oil
- Salt-pepper

Arní me Damáskina

LAMB WITH PLUMS

5 - 6 SERVINGS

- 1 ½ kilos (3 lbs 6 oz) lamb
- 1 onion, sliced
- 300 grams (10 oz) almonds, crushed
- 2 tablespoons butter
- 1 tablespoon flour
- 2 lemons
- 2 tablespoons sugar
- 800 grams (1 lb 12 oz) plums
- Salt-pepper

Wash the lamb, strain and cut it into small portions. Place the meat portions in a bowl, add salt and pepper, the onion and the juice of one lemon and marinate for an hour. Drain the lamb and sauté it in a pot with butter. Next, add the flour to the pot and stir with a wooden spoon. Add a small amount of water and the liquid from the bowl. Cook over a medium fire. When the lamb is half cooked, add the almonds and the plums. Cover the pot and continue cooking on low heat, until the meat and the plums are done.

Finally, add the sugar and the juice of the other lemon. Serve hot.

Moschári Ragoú me Makarónia

BEEF RAGOUT WITH MACARONI

5 - 6 SERVINGS

◇ 2 kilos (4 lbs 8 oz) beef

◇ Olive oil

◇ 3-4 cloves garlic

◇ 1 ½ teacups Kefalotyri or Parmesan cheese, grated

◇ 2 grated onions

◇ 2-3 bay leaves

◇ Cinnamon, cloves, allspice

◇ 2 tablespoons tomato paste or 2 teacups tomato juice without seeds

◇ 50 grams (2 oz) spicy cheese

◇ 1 kilo (2 lbs 4 oz) thick macaroni

◇ Butter

◇ Salt-pepper

Wash and strain the beef and cut it into portions. Make deeps slits with a sharp knife at the meet pieces and insert the chopped garlic and pieces of the spicy cheese. Tie each portion with string and season with salt and pepper. Heat the oil in a pot and sauté the meat pieces, until they are golden. Cover the sautéed meat with water.

Add the tomato, the onions, the bay leaves and all the spice. Cover the pot and cook until the ingredients are left only in their own broth (which is thick and tasty). In another pot boil the macaroni in plenty of salted water. When they are ready, drain them and scald them with butter. Serve the macaroni onto dishes. Pour the beef broth over them and put one or two pieces of meat on each plate (the string should be removed from each piece before cooking). Sprinkle with cinnamon and grated Kefalotyri or Parmesan cheese.

Hirinó me Kástana

PORK WITH CHESTNUTS

Cook the chestnuts in a pot and remove their inner and outer coverings (shell and skin). Wash and strain the meat and cut it into portions. Heat some oil in a pot and sauté the pork in it, until it turns golden brown. Add the finely diced onion, salt and pepper and sauté a little while longer.

Dissolve the tomato paste in a glass of water and pour it over the meat. Lower the fire and allow the food to cook. When the meat is done, add the chestnuts and continue cooking for another 3-4 minutes. Serve immediately.

5 - 6 SERVINGS

◇ 1 ½ kilos (3 lbs 6 oz) lean leg of pork

◇ 1 ½ kilos (3 lbs 6 oz) large chestnuts

◇ 1 onion, finely diced

◇ 1 tablespoon tomato paste

◇ Olive oil

◇ Salt-pepper

Arnáki Frikassé me Maroúli

LAMB FRICASSEE
WITH COS (ROMAINE) LETTUCE

5 - 6 SERVINGS

◇ 1 kilo (2 lbs 4 oz) lamb

◇ 4 Cos (Romaine) lettuces, coarsely cut

◇ 3 spring onions, coarsely cut

◇ 1 onion

◇ 1 teacup olive oil

◇ 2 tablespoons flour

◇ Some dill and parsley

◇ 3 egg yolks

◇ The juice of two lemons

◇ 1 tablespoon cornflour

◇ Salt-pepper

Wash and strain the lamb, cut it into servings and scald it. Cool it down with water and let it drain.

Place the oil in a pot and sauté the onion. Add the lamb and the flour and sauté stirring constantly, until the flour changes colour. Add some water, salt, pepper, the parsley and the dill. Let these boil for about 15 minutes.

In a large pot, place the lamb, drained, on one side and the lettuces and the spring onions (which have been scalded) on the other. Purée the sauce (which has been previously cooked with the meat) and add it to pot with the lamb, the lettuces, and the spring onions. Boil these together for 15 minutes. Remove the pot from the fire. Prepare an egg and lemon sauce by beating the egg yolks, the cornflour, the lemon juice and some broth from the pot. Pour the egg and lemon sauce over the meat stirring lightly. Finally put the pot back on a very low heat for 5 minutes shaking the pot from time to time so that the egg does not solidify; on no account let the food boil after the egg and lemon sauce has been added, because it will curdle.

◁ *Lamb with Strained Yoghurt Sauce*

◁ *Lamb Fricassee with Field Vegetables*

Arnáki Frikassé me Araká

LAMB FRICASSEE WITH GREEN PEAS

Wash and strain the lamb and cut it into portions. Heat half the butter in a pot and add the lamb pieces, the sliced carrot and the finely sliced onions. Sauté lightly. Next add the finely chopped dill, salt and pepper, cover with water and cook for an hour. Then add the green peas, shelled (in case they are fresh) and washed. Cover the pot and cook until peas are done. Place the remaining butter in a small pot. Add the flour and mix with a small amount of broth from the lamb and peas.

When this mixture boils, remove it from the fire and add the eggs (beaten) and the lemon juice beating constantly.

Pour the egg and lemon sauce over the lamb and shake the pot a few times to help the sauce spread. Serve hot.

5-6 SERVINGS
◇ 1 ½ kilos (3 lbs 6 oz) lamb
◇ 1 ½ kilos (3 lbs 6 oz) green peas
◇ 1 teacup butter
◇ 1 carrot
◇ 2-3 spring onions
◇ Dill, finely chopped
◇ 1 tablespoon flour
◇ 3 eggs, beaten
◇ 3 lemons
◇ Salt-pepper

Hirinó me Prása

PORK WITH LEEKS

4-5 SERVINGS
◇ 1 ½ kilos (3 lbs 6 oz) lean pork leg
◇ 2 kilos (4 lbs 8 oz) leeks
◇ 1 glass red wine
◇ 2 eggs
◇ Olive oil
◇ Salt-pepper
◇ The juice of one lemon

Wash the pork, cut it into portions and drain. Heat some oil in a pot and sauté the meat in it. When the meat looks golden brown, pour in the wine and season with salt and pepper.

In the meantime, top and tail the leeks, discard the coarse leaves, rinse and slit them down the middle. Add the leeks to the pot with the meat and let them cook in their own liquid (water). Add some water, if needed. When the leeks are done, prepare an egg and lemon sauce (see p. 50) and pour it over the food. Serve hot.

Arnáki Frikassé me Agria Hórta

LAMB FRICASSEE WITH FIELD VEGETABLES

6 SERVINGS

◇ 6 servings lamb (1 ½ kilos approx. or 3 lbs 6 oz)

◇ 3-4 spring onions, finely chopped

◇ 1 kilo (2 lbs 4 oz) field vegetables, e.g. dandelions

◇ 1 teacup olive oil

◇ 2 eggs

◇ 2 tablespoons ground dill

◇ The juice of two lemons

◇ 2 tablespoons cornflour

◇ Salt-pepper

Heat the oil in a pot and sauté the onions over a medium fire. Add the lamb which has been cut into small servings and season with salt and pepper. Pour in an amount of water and let the lamb boil for about an hour and a half.

Clean the vegetables and wash them very well. Place them on one side of the pot with the lamb, sprinkle over with the dill and allow everything to boil for another 20-25 minutes. Remove the pot from the fire and prepare the egg and lemon sauce as follows:

Beat the egg whites in a bowl, then, gradually add the egg yolks, the cornflour, the lemon juice and, finally, enough broth from the meat beating all the time. Pour the egg and lemon sauce over the food, rotating the pot a few times. Serve hot.

Note: do not reheat the pot after the egg and lemon sauce has been added, because the sauce will curdle.

Arnáki Psiméno se Karvéli Psomí

LAMB BAKED IN A LOAF OF BREAD

Wash the lamb and let it strain. Season it with salt and pepper. Sprinkle with oregano and spread butter and mustard over it.

Cut the bread horizontally (exactly) down the centre. Butter the bread and place the lamb in it (as in a pan). Cover the meat with the other half of bread and wrap in waxed paper. Tie the bundle and bake for about 2 1/2 hours in a medium oven. Cut into portions and serve hot with fried potatoes.

5-6 SERVINGS

◇ 1 ½ kilos (3 lbs 6 oz) leg of lamb

◇ 1 spoonful mustard

◇ Oregano

◇ 2-3 spoonfuls butter

◇ 1 large loaf of bread

◇ Waxed paper

◇ Salt-pepper

Souvláki me Píta

LAMB KEBAB WITH PITA

Cut the pork into small cubes.
Place it in a bowl with salt, pepper, oregano and oil. Lift the meat out and thread it on small wooden skewers. Cook under a hot grill on both sides (about 7 minutes on each side). Heat the «pita» bread. Remove the grilled pork from the skewers and place an appropriate amount of it on each «pita» bread, along with some onion, parsley, slices of tomato, salt, pepper and some «tzatziki», if desired. Serve warm on individual dishes.

Note: Pork can be replaced with beef, if preferred.

5-6 SERVINGS

◇ 1 kilo (2 lbs 4 oz) pork
◇ 12 «pita» bread
◇ 2-3 tomatoes, sliced
◇ 2 onions, sliced
◇ 1 teacup olive oil
◇ 2 tablespoons parsley, finely chopped
◇ Salt-pepper
◇ Oregano
◇ «Tzatziki» (see p. 73)

Hirinó me Sélino Avgolémono

PORK WITH CELERY IN EGG AND LEMON SAUCE

Pork with Celery in Egg and Lemon Sauce ➤

Lamb Kebab with Pita ➤

Wash and strain the meat. In a pot, sauté the onions in the oil. Add the pork, which has been cut in small servings, salt, pepper and some water and allow it to boil for about an hour and a half. Then clean the celery, cut it in large pieces, wash it well and add it to the pork along with the dill. Allow everything to boil for another 35 minutes. Remove the pot from the fire.

In a bowl, beat the egg whites first. While continuing to beat, gradually add the yolks, the cornflour, the lemon juice, and some broth from the pot. Pour the egg and lemon sauce over the meat shaking the pot a few times to ensure that the sauce spreads everywhere. Serve hot.

6 SERVINGS

◇ 6 servings (1-1½ kilos or 2 lbs 4 oz - 3 lbs 6 oz) pork
◇ 1 kilo (2 lbs 4 oz) celery
◇ 1 teacup olive oil
◇ 2-3 spring onions
◇ 2 tablespoons dill, finely chopped
◇ 2 eggs
◇ 2 lemons
◇ 1 tablespoon cornflour
◇ Salt-pepper

Moschári me Pouré apó Melitzánes

BEEF WITH MASHED AUBERGINES (EGGPLANTS)

5-6 SERVINGS

- ✧ 2 kilos (4 lbs 8 oz) aubergines (eggplants)
- ✧ 1 kilo (2 lbs 4 oz) beef, deboned
- ✧ 1 teacup olive oil
- ✧ 1 teacup butter
- ✧ ½ kilo (1 lb 2 oz) tomatoes, peeled and finely diced
- ✧ 1 teacup milk
- ✧ 1 glass wine
- ✧ 2 onions, grated
- ✧ 2 bay leaves
- ✧ 2 tablespoons flour
- ✧ Salt-pepper

Wash and strain the beef and cut it into small pieces. Scald some oil in a pot and brown the beef and the onions in it.

Pour in the wine. Add the tomatoes, salt and pepper and the bay leaves and cook.

Put the aubergines (eggplants) in a pan and bake in the oven for about ½ hour.

When the aubergines (eggplants) are ready, let them cool. Peel them and remove their seeds. Mash the remaining pulp.

In another pot, heat the butter, add the flour and pour in the milk stirring constantly. When this sauce thickens, pour it into the aubergine pulp mash. Serve the meat in individual portions on dishes. Pour the meat's broth over the meat and place some of the aubergine mash next to the meat.

Moschári me Loukánika Youvétsi

BEEF AND SAUSAGES CASSEROLE

5-6 SERVINGS

- ✧ 1 kilo (2 lbs 4 oz) beef
- ✧ 3-4 Italian or Greek style sausages
- ✧ 1 large onion, finely chopped
- ✧ 150 grams (5 oz) butter
- ✧ 100 grams (3 ½ oz) olive oil
- ✧ 1 kilo (2 lbs 4 oz) tomatoes, finely diced
- ✧ 500 grams (1 lb 2 oz) «kritharaki» (orzo), a rice-shaped pasta
- ✧ Salt-pepper
- ✧ Aluminum foil

Wash and stain the beef and cut it into portions. Sauté it in a pot with oil and butter, until it turns golden. Add the sausages (sliced) and the onion and stir with a wooden spoon. Season with salt and pepper and lower the fire. Line the bottom and sides of a pan with aluminum foil and empty the contents of the pot into it. Add the pasta, the tomatoes, salt and pepper and stir with a wooden spoon. Finally, cover the whole surface of the pan with aluminum foil and bake at 200-230 degrees for about 1 ½ hours.

Hirinó me Plygoúri ke Revíthia

PORK WITH «PLYGOURI» (CRACKED WHEAT) AND CHICK PEAS

Wash and strain the meat. Soak the chick peas in salted water with the baking soda overnight. In the morning rub them well with salt to remove their skins. Rinse the peas, drain them and put them in a pot with the meat.

4 - 5 SERVINGS
- ◇ 1 kilo (2 lbs 4 oz) lean pork, cut into portions
- ◇ ½ teacup butter
- ◇ ½ teacup «plygouri» (cracked wheat, finely chopped)
- ◇ 1 teacup chick-peas
- ◇ Salt-cinnamon
- ◇ 1 teaspoon baking soda (optional)

Cover with water, season with salt and cook. While cooking add water, if needed. You should be left with about three teacups of broth, when the cooking is done.

Pour this broth into another pot and bring to a boil. Add the «plygouri» (cracked wheat), season with salt and cook until all the liquid is absorbed. Heat the butter in a frying-pan until boiling, pour over the cracked wheat, cover the pot and allow for the liquid to be absorbed.

Finally, serve the cracked wheat on a platter. Garnish it with the meat and the chick peas. Sprinkle with cinnamon.

Hirinó me Fassólia

PORK WITH GREEN BEANS

Wash and strain the pork and cut it into portions. Heat some oil in a pot and sauté the meat and onion in it.

5 - 6 SERVINGS
- ◇ 2 kilos (4 lbs 8 oz) pork
- ◇ 1 ½ kilos (3 lbs 6 oz) green beans
- ◇ 1 ½ teacups tomato juice
- ◇ 1 onion, finely diced
- ◇ ½ teacup olive oil
- ◇ Salt-pepper
- ◇ Some celery

Pour in the tomato juice, salt and pepper and let them cook.

In the meantime, you have boiled the green beans and the celery in salted water and have drained them. (Have in mind that the beans should not be well done).

When the pork is almost done, add the green beans and cook these together for a few minutes. Serve hot.

Note: *This is a rich dish. It is suggested, therefore, only for winter noon meals.*

Moschári stifádo

BEEF RAGOUT WITH ONIONS, VINEGAR AND TOMATO SAUCE

6 SERVINGS

- ✧ 6 servings beef (1 ½ kilos approx. or 3 lbs 6 oz)
- ✧ 1 kilo small onions (2 lbs 4 oz)
- ✧ 1 teacup olive oil
- ✧ 1 teacup vinegar
- ✧ 2-3 ripe tomatoes
- ✧ Rosemary
- ✧ 1 bay leaf
- ✧ 2 cloves garlic
- ✧ Salt - Pepper corns

Wash and strain the meat pieces.

In a pot, heat the olive oil over a medium fire and brown the meat. Add the onions and allow these to sauté for about 5 minutes.

Add the vinegar, the tomatoes (finely diced), the garlic, the rosemary, salt, pepper, the bay leaf and an amount of water.

Allow the ragout to boil for about two hours, until it is left in its own sauce.

Serve hot.

◄ Beef with Green Olives

◄ Beef Ragout with Onions, Vinegar and Tomato Sauce

Moscharáki me Prássines Eliés

BEEF WITH GREEN OLIVES

6 SERVINGS

- ✧ 6 servings beef (1 ½ kilos approx. or 3 lbs 6 oz)
- ✧ 1 kilo green olives (2 lbs 4 oz)
- ✧ 2-3 ripe tomatoes, finely diced
- ✧ 1-2 onions, finely chopped
- ✧ 1 teacup olive oil
- ✧ Salt-pepper
- ✧ 1 glass red wine

Wash and strain the meat and cut it into small pieces (2 pieces per serving). Heat the oil in a pot and sauté the onion. Add the meat and allow it to sauté for five minutes while stirring.

Pour in the red wine, add the tomatoes, salt, pepper and the olives (they have been pitted and scalded). Add some water and allow all to boil for about 2 hours over a medium fire. Serve hot.

Arnáki sto Foúrno me Spanakóryzo

BAKED LAMB WITH SPINACH RICE

MANY SERVINGS

◇ 3-4 kilos (6 lbs 12 oz 9 lbs) lamb
◇ 2 kilos (4 lbs 8 oz) spinach
◇ 1 kilo (2 lbs 4 oz) spring onions, chopped
◇ 6 teacups intestines and liver (both finely chopped)
◇ 4 teacups rice, washed
◇ 1 teacup butter
◇ Mint
◇ ½ teacup olive oil
◇ Salt - Red and black pepper

Wash the lamb well, strain and season with salt and pepper. Place it in a pan, pour melted butter over it and place the pan in pre-heated oven.

Wash the spinach meticulously and shred it in small pieces. Scald some oil in a pot and sauté the onions in it. Add the spinach, season with red pepper and sauté. Put the sautéed spinach and onions into the pan with the lamb. Add the intestines (cleaned and washed as described on p. 38) and liver (slightly boiled), the salt, the black pepper, the mint and a little bit of water.

Return the pan to the oven and continue baking. When the water in the pan starts boiling, add the rice. Continue baking for 1 ½ to 2 hours (approximately). Serve hot.

Arnáki me Sparángia

LAMB WITH ASPARAGUS

Wash and strain the lamb and cut it into portions. Sauté it in scalding oil with the onions, until they turn golden.

Add some water and continue cooking until the lamb is half done.

Prepare and wash the asparagus. Scald them in boiling water; strain them and add them to the lamb. Season with salt and cook over a low fire until the lamb and the asparagus are done.

Remove the pot from the fire. Take a teacup of broth form the pot.

Squeeze the juice of one lemon into the broth and add the cornflour. Return the broth to the pot and shake the pot a few times. Place the pot over the fire again for 2-3 minutes and season with pepper. Serve as soon as the sauce thickens.

5-6 SERVINGS

◇ 1 ½ kilos (3 lbs 6 oz) lamb
◇ 1 ½ kilos (3 lbs 6 oz) asparagus
◇ 1 teacup olive oil
◇ 2 onions, finely diced
◇ 1 lemon
◇ 1 tablespoon cornflour
◇ Salt-pepper

Arnáki a la Kléftra

LAMB WITH YOGHURT SAUCE

5 - 6 SERVINGS

- ◇ 1 kilo of lamb
- ◇ 4-5 spring onions, coarsely chopped
- ◇ 1 teacup olive oil
- ◇ 2 teacups strained yoghurt
- ◇ Pinch of thyme
- ◇ Salt-pepper
- ◇ Small amount of dill, finely chopped
- ◇ 4 pieces of waxed paper, cut into long strips of about 20 cm width, each

Wash and strain the lamb and cut it into servings. Scald it, allow it to cool and place it in a bowl.

Sauté the onions in the oil. Add the salt and pepper, the oregano, the thyme, the dill and the yoghurt. Let this mixture stand for approximately 30 minutes, to allow the aroma of the various ingredients to mix.

Proceed by wrapping the servings in the waxed paper as follows;

Spread the pieces of waxed paper on a table (or counter). On one end of each strip place one serving of lamb and cover it with a appropriate amount of the prepared yoghurt. Then wrap the waxed paper containing the lamb and mixture into tight bundles, as is done with «dolmadakia». Ensure that each piece of lamb is totally covered with the yoghurt mixture.

Arrange the bundles in an oiled pan and bake in a medium oven for about two hours. Serve hot while the lamb is still wrapped in the waxed paper.

Arní Xydáto sto Tigáni

FRIED LAMB IN VINEGAR

Pound the lamb slices with a pestle. Wash and strain them. Coat them with flour and fry them on both sides in a mixture of half the butter and half the oil for frying. When the meat slices are done, put them in a pot and leave them aside.

Filter the remains of the oil and butter being careful to omit any burnt sediment. Pour in the vinegar (which contains a spoonful of flour), the finely chopped garlic and season to taste. Cook until the sauce thickens up, pour in over the lamb and bring the pot to the boil. Be careful to avoid sticking. (Shake from time to time). Add a slight amount of water. Serve hot with fried potatoes.

4 - 5 SERVINGS

- ◇ 1 leg of lamb, sliced
- ◇ 1 teacup vinegar
- ◇ 2-3 spoonfuls flour
- ◇ ½ grass oil for frying
- ◇ 2 spoonfuls butter
- ◇ 4-5 cloves garlic
- ◇ Salt-pepper

Minced meat

- *Stuffed Cabbage Leaves*
- *Tomatoes Stuffed*
- *Minced Meat Rissoles, Smyrna Style*
- *«Moussaka» with Aubergines*

Moussakás me Melitzánes

«MOUSSAKA» WITH AUBERGINES

Heat the cup of oil in a pot and sauté the chopped onions in it. Add the minced meat and continue to sauté for another 10 minutes. Next, add the tomatoes, the garlic, the bay leaf and the salt and pepper and allow the mixture to boil for approximately one hour. In the meantime, wash the aubergines (eggplants) and trim off their stems.

Then cut them in round slices and let them soak in salted water for about an hour (to remove their bitter juices).

Drain the aubergine slices, coat them with flour and fry them in very hot oil. In a pan, place a layer of aubergine slices, salt and pepper and a layer of the minced meat mixture (also drained to remove excess liquid). Add another layer of aubergines and minced meat mixture. Finally, pour the béchamel sauce (of medium consistency) over the last layer. Sprinkle with the grated cheese and bake at a high temperature for approximately 20-25 minutes. Take out the «mousaka» and cut it in square pieces. Serve hot.

5 - 6 SERVINGS

- ◇ 4-5 aubergines (eggplants)
- ◇ ½ kilo (1 lb 2 oz) minced meat
- ◇ 2-3 tomatoes
- ◇ 1 teacup olive oil
- ◇ 2 onions, finely chopped
- ◇ 1 bay leaf
- ◇ 1 garlic clove
- ◇ Oil for frying
- ◇ ½ teacup grated Parmesan cheese
- ◇ Some flour
- ◇ 3 teacups Béchamel sauce (see p. 57)

Domátes Yemistés me Kymá ke Ryzi

TOMATOES STUFFED
WITH MINCED MEAT AND RICE

Wash the tomatoes, cut a thin round slice off the top, stem end of each one with a sharp knife and keep them aside. With a teaspoon, scoop most of the tomato pulp out and shred it finely.

Next, prepare the stuffing as follows:

Heat the oil in a cooking pan and sauté the onions in it, until they look brown. Add the minced meat and let it sauté for another 10 minutes, stirring with a spoon all the time. Add the tomato pulp, salt, pepper, the parsley, the mint, some water and let them boil for about 1 hour.

Finally, add the rice –washed and strained– and continue boiling for a further 10 minutes.

Fill the tomatoes, which you have arranged in a baking pan or a pyrex dish, with the prepared stuffing.

Be careful not to overfill them.

Pour some tomato juice in the dish, and fill the gaps between the stuffed tomatoes with potatoes, cut in slices.

Season to taste and bake in a medium oven for about 40-45 minutes.

6 SERVINGS

- ◇ 12 ripe tomatoes
- ◇ ½ kilo (1 lb 2 oz) minced meat
- ◇ 2 teacups rice
- ◇ 2 onions, finely chopped
- ◇ 1 ½ teacups olive oil
- ◇ 2 tablespoons parsley, finely chopped
- ◇ 1 teaspoon mint, finely chopped
- ◇ Salt-pepper

Youvarlákia Avgolémono

MINCED MEAT RISSOLES
IN EGG AND LEMON SAUCE

In a bowl, place the minced meat, the salt and pepper, the parsley, 2 eggs, the grated onions and the rice. Mix these ingredients together well. Pour 3 water –glasses of water– or beef broth in a pot and bring it to a boil over a medium fire. In the meantime, shape the meat mixture into round shapes and drop them into the boiling broth (or water).

Allow the meatballs to simmer for about an hour and a half. Add water, if needed. Remove the pot from the fire and prepare the egg and lemon sauce as follows:

In a bowl, beat the whites of the remaining eggs first and add the yolks next. Gradually add the lemon juice, the cornflour and some broth from the pot beating all the time. Pour the egg and lemon sauce over the meatballs. Slightly shake the pot a few times to be sure that the sauce spreads throughout the pot. Serve the meatballs hot.

Note:

On no account let the food boil after the egg and lemon sauce has been added, because the sauce might curdle.

6 SERVINGS

◇ 1 kilo (1 lb 2 oz) minced meat

◇ 2 teacups rice, washed and strained

◇ 2 onions, grated

◇ 1 teacup olive oil

◇ 2 tablespoons, finely chopped parsley

◇ The juice of two lemons

◇ 4 eggs

◇ 1 tablespoon cornflour

◇ Salt-pepper

Lahanodolmádes

STUFFED CABBAGE LEAVES

In a large bowl, place the minced meat, the rice, the parsley, the dill, the very finely chopped onions, and the salt and pepper. Mix these together well. Clean the cabbage discarding the heart and the tough outer leaves. Bring a pot of water to a boil and scald the cabbage for 5 minutes. When the cabbage is cold enough to handle, separate the leaves, cutting the very large ones in half.

Place a small quantity of the meat mixture on one edge of each leaf. Now fold each leaf in such a way so as to retain the mixture in the leaf. Line the bottom of a large pot with cabbage leaves and place the stuffed leaves in circles. When all the stuffed leaves have been placed in the pot, add some water, the oil and lay an inverted plate over the stuffed leaves (so they do not come apart while cooking). Allow them to boil on medium heat for about an hour and a half. Remove the pot from the fire.

5 - 6 SERVINGS
◇ 1 kilo (2 lbs 3 oz) minced meat
◇ 1 medium-sized cabbage
◇ 2 onions, finely chopped
◇ 2 tablespoons finely chopped parsley
◇ 1 teacup olive oil
◇ 2 tablespoons dill, finely chopped
◇ 1 teacup rice
◇ 2 eggs
◇ 2 lemons (the juice)
◇ Salt-pepper
◇ 1 tablespoon cornflour

Prepare the egg and lemon sauce as follows:
In a bowl, beat the egg whites, until they are stiff, gradually add –while you continue to beat– the yolks, the lemon juice, the cornflour and finally some broth from the pot. When the sauce is ready, pour it over the stuffed leaves. Gently shake the pot a few times to make sure that the sauce spreads everywhere. Serve immediately without reheating the food.

Keftédes Tiganití me Sáltsa Domátas

FRIED MINCED MEAT RISSOLES
IN TOMATO SAUCE

5-6 SERVINGS
- 1 kilo (2 lbs 4 oz) minced beef
- 2 onions, grated
- 2 eggs
- 1 teacup olive oil
- 2-3 slices bread
- 2 tablespoons chopped parsley
- 1 clove garlic
- Salt, pepper
- Oil for frying
- Some flour
- 3 teacups tomato sauce (see p. 55)

Place the minced meat in a bowl and add the eggs, the parsley, the garlic and the grated onions. Soak the bread and squeeze excess moisture. Add it to the meat mixture along with salt and pepper. Mix all the ingredients well. Make small round shapes and flatten them by hand until they are about one centimetre thick.
Coat the meatballs lightly with flour and fry them in very hot oil.
Place the fried meatballs in a pan with the prepared tomato sauce. Allow them to cook for about 15 minutes over a medium fire. Serve the meat balls hot, garnished with fried potatoes or rice.

Melitzánes «Papoutsákia»

STUFFED AUBERGINES
«LITTLE SHOES» STYLE

Fried Minced Meat Rissoles ➢

Minced Meat Rissoles in Egg and Lemon Sauce ➢

Stuffed Aubergines ➢

Lightly sauté the onions in the oil. Add the minced meat and sauté for 10 minutes stirring constantly. Add the tomatoes, the garlic, the bay leaf, salt pepper and a small amount for water and allow the mixture to simmer for about an hour.
In the meantime, wash the aubergines and slice them in two, lengthwise. With a sharp knife make incisions down their centre and place the aubergines in salted water for about an hour. Next, drain the aubergines, fry them in very hot oil and arrange pulp and add it to the meat mixture. Fill the aubergine halves with this mixture and cover them with thick béchamel sauce (see p. 57). Sprinkle the stuffed aubergines or the «little shoes» –as they are called– with grated Parmesan cheese and bake them in a medium oven for about 25 minutes.

6 SERVINGS
- 6 aubergines (round)
- ½ kilo (1 lb 2 oz) minced meat
- 2-3 ripe tomatoes, diced
- 2 onions, finely diced
- 1 teacup olive oil
- 1 bay leaf
- 1 clove garlic
- Salt-pepper
- Oil for frying
- Parmesan cheese, grated

Soutzoukákia Smyrnáyka

MINCED MEAT RISSOLES, SMYRNA STYLE

4 - 5 SERVINGS
- ◇ 2 slices bread, soaked in water
- ◇ ½ teacup butter or olive oil
- ◇ 2 cloves garlic
- ◇ 4 medium-sized tomatoes
- ◇ 2 tablespoons butter
- ◇ 1 egg, beaten
- ◇ ½ kilo (1 lb 2 oz) minced meat
- ◇ ½ teacup red wine
- ◇ Salt-pepper
- ◇ Cumin
- ◇ A pinch of sugar

Squeeze excess moisture from the soaked bread. Place it in a bowl and add the cumin, the egg, some olive oil, the minced meat, salt and pepper. Mix well by hand and make about 20 cylindrically shaped meatballs. In a frying pan, heat the oil until boiling and fry the «soutzoukakia».

Prepare a tomato sauce as follows:
Wash the tomatoes, cut them up and purée them. Empty the tomatoes into a pot and add the butter, the salt, the pepper, a bit of sugar and the wine. Cook the sauce for about half an hour. Put the «soutzoukakia» into the pot with the sauce and cook over a low fire for a further 15 minutes. Serve hot.

Angináres Yemistés me Kymá

ARTICHOKES STUFFED WITH MINCED MEAT

Clean the artichokes, by cutting their stalks and peeling the tough outer leaves. Cut the tips of the remaining leaves off and remove the «hairy inside» in the middle of the heart with a teaspoon. Rub the artichokes with a lemon cup, drop them in a pot and cover them with water. Add the juice of one lemon, season with salt and cook for about 20 minutes.

5 - 6 SERVINGS
- ◇ 12 large artichokes
- ◇ ½ teacup butter
- ◇ 1 medium-sized onion, finely diced
- ◇ ½ kilo (1 lb 2 oz) minced meat
- ◇ Salt-pepper
- ◇ The juice of one lemon
- ◇ Parsley, finely chopped
- ◇ 1 ½ tablespoons toasted breadcrumbs
- ◇ 2 eggs
- ◇ Béchamel sauce (see p.57)
- ◇ ½ teacup grated cheese

Remove the artichokes from the pot, drain them and lay them in a buttered pan.

Sauté the onion lightly in a frying pan containing the butter. Add the minced meat, salt, pepper and the finely chopped parsley. Sauté for a few minutes.

Remove the frying pan from the fire. Add the breadcrumbs and the one egg, beaten, and stir well. Stuff the artichokes with the minced meat mixture.

Prepare a batch of béchamel sauce (following the recipe on p.57) and add to it the other egg (beaten) and the grated cheese.

Cover each stuffed artichoke with the sauce and bake them for about 40 minutes in a medium fire. Serve hot.

Roló apó Kymá

MINCED MEAT ROLL

In a bowl, place the drained bread the minced meat, the wine, ½ teacup water, the onion, the beaten egg, salt and pepper, the finely chopped parsley and four tablespoons butter. Mix well by hand making sure that the bread is incorporated. Then place the mixture on a damp piece of waxed paper, and shape it into a rectangle. Down the centre of the rectangle line the boiled eggs. Wrap the mixture around the eggs. Wrap the waxed paper around the meat roll and secure the two ends. Butter a pan and place in it the meat roll which has been oiled. Bake in strong oven for half an hour. Remove the waxed paper and continue cooking in a medium oven, until the roll turns golden brown.

In the meantime, prepare a tomato sauce as follows:

Boil the tomato juice for 5 minutes with half a teacup of water, the garlic, the sugar, salt and pepper and two tablespoons olive oil. Pour the sauce over the meat roll and continue cooking for another ½ hour. Serve sliced, hot or cold.

4 - 5 SERVINGS

- ◇ 650 grams (1 lb 8 oz) minced meat
- ◇ 3 slices bread, medium-sized, without crust, soaked in water
- ◇ ½ teacup red wine
- ◇ 1 medium-sized onion, finely diced
- ◇ 1 egg, beaten
- ◇ Salt-pepper
- ◇ Parsley, finely chopped
- ◇ ½ teacup melted butter
- ◇ 6 hardboiled eggs, shelled
- ◇ 1 ½ teacups tomato juice
- ◇ 2 cloves garlic, crushed
- ◇ Olive oil
- ◇ A pinch of sugar
- ◇ Waxed paper

Poultry

- *Chicken with Rice and Tomato Sauce*

- *Chicken with Leeks and Sausages*

- *Chicken with Olives and Red Peppers*

- *Stuffed Chicken, Oriental Style*

Kotópoulo Yemistó Orientál

STUFFED CHICKEN, ORIENTAL STYLE

4-5 SERVINGS

◇ 1 large chicken

◇ 100 grams (3 ½ oz) vermicelli

◇ 1 cup long-grain rice

◇ 250 grams (9 oz) chestnuts, peeled

◇ 1 teacup olive oil

◇ 1 teacup raisins

◇ 100 grams (3 ½ oz) bird liver (optional)

◇ 1 onion, finely diced

◇ 1 clove garlic

◇ Salt-pepper

Prepare the stuffing as follows:

Heat the oil in a pot over a medium fire. Add the vermicelli and allow it to turn golden.

Add the bird liver, the chestnuts, the raisins, the onion, and the rice constantly stirring. Let everything sauté for about 10 minutes. Pour in two cups of water and continue cooking for another 10 minutes. Prepare the chicken by seasoning with salt and pepper and crushed garlic. Fill the chicken's inside with the prepared stuffing.

Sew up the chicken and place it in a pyrex pan. If you have leftover stuffing, place it in the pan alongside the chicken. Bake in a medium oven for about an hour and a half. Add some water, if necessary. Serve hot.

Kotópoulo me Eliés ke Kókines Piperiés

CHICKEN WITH OLIVES AND RED PEPPERS

6 SERVINGS

◇ 6 portions chicken

◇ 3-4 red peppers, cut in large pieces

◇ 250 grams (9 oz) black olives

◇ 2-3 ripe tomatoes, finely diced

◇ 1 glass red wine

◇ 2 onions, finely diced

◇ 1 ½ teacups olive oil

◇ Salt-pepper

◇ Pinch of thyme

In a pot, heat the oil, add the chicken portions and brown for about 10 minutes.

Add the onions, the peppers and the olives while stirring. Pour in the wine. Next, add the tomatoes, the thyme, the salt and pepper and an amount of water. Continue cooking over a medium fire for about an hour and a half. Serve hot as a second course.

Kotópoulo me Prásso ke Loukánika

CHICKEN WITH LEEKS AND SAUSAGES

6 SERVINGS

◇ 6 portions chicken

◇ 250 grams (9 oz) carrots, coarsely chopped

◇ 200 grams (7 oz) sausages, thickly sliced

◇ 1 teacup olive oil

◇ 1 ripe tomato, finely diced

◇ 1 glass red wine

◇ Salt-pepper

◇ 3-4 leeks

Heat the oil in a pot over a medium fire. Add the chicken portions and the sausages and let them brown for about 10 minutes.

Next, pour in the wine, add the tomatoes, salt, pepper and some water. Allow everything to boil for about an hour.

Finally, add the carrots and the leeks and continue cooking for another half an hour. Serve hot as a second course.

Kotópoulo «Atzém» Piláfi

CHICKEN WITH RICE AND TOMATO SAUCE

In a pot, sauté the onions in the olive oil for about 5 minutes. Add the chicken portions and let them turn golden brown.

Next, add the tomatoes and some water, salt and pepper and let everything cook for about an hour and a half. Add the rice. Make sure that for every cup of rice there are two cups of broth in the pot (approximately). Continue to cook for another 15 minutes. Serve hot as a second course.

6 SERVINGS

◇ 6 portions chicken

◇ ½ kilo (1 lb 2 oz) long-grain rice

◇ 3-4 ripe tomatoes, finely diced

◇ 1-2 onions, finely diced

◇ 1 teacup olive oil

◇ Salt-pepper

Kókoras i Kotópoulo Krassáto

ROOSTER OR CHICKEN IN WINE

Heat the oil in a pot and brown the chicken for about 10 minutes.
Pour in the wine, add the vegetables, salt and pepper and the appropriate amount of water. Cook over a medium fire for about an hour and a half. Check the pot, while cooking, and add water, if needed. Serve hot as a second course.

6 SERVINGS
◇ 6 portions chicken
◇ 200 grams (7 oz) mushrooms, quartered
◇ 200 grams (7 oz) small onions, peeled
◇ 1 glass red wine
◇ 1 teacup olive oil
◇ Salt-pepper

Rooster or Chicken in Wine ➤

Chicken with Carrots and Onions ➤

Chicken with Noodles (Hylopites) ➤

Kotópoulo me Karóto ke Kremydia

CHICKEN WITH CARROTS AND ONIONS

6 SERVINGS
◇ 6 portions chicken
◇ 250 grams (9 oz) onions, roughly chopped
◇ 250 grams (9 oz) carrots, thickly sliced
◇ 1 teacup olive oil
◇ Salt-pepper
◇ 1 glass white wine

In a pot, heat the oil over a medium fire and add the chicken pieces. Brown them for about 10 minutes. Pour in the wine and add the onions, the carrots, the salt and pepper and the appropriate amount of water. Cook over a medium fire for about an hour and a half. Serve hot as a second course.

Kotópoulo me Hylopítes

CHICKEN WITH NOODLES (HYLOPITES)

6 SERVINGS

◇ 6 portions chicken

◇ ½ kilo (1 lb 2 oz) noodles

◇ 3-4 ripe tomatoes, finely diced

◇ 2-3 onions, finely chopped

◇ 1 teacup olive oil

◇ Salt-pepper

Pour the oil into a pot and sauté the onions for about 5 minutes over a medium fire.

Next, add the chicken portions and cook for 5 minutes while constantly stirring. Add the tomatoes, salt and pepper, and the appropriate amount of water. Cook for another 45 minutes. Finally, add the noodles (1 part noodles, 3 parts liquid), see page (p.) and continue cooking for another 15 minutes. Serve hot as a second course.

Papí me Patátes ke Kástana

DUCK WITH POTATOES AND CHESTNUTS

Clean and wash the duck. Drain it and season with salt and pepper. Boil the chestnuts and remove both their outer and inner coverings (shell and skin). Break the almonds into big pieces and mix them with the raisins, the chestnuts, the butter, salt and pepper. Stuff the duck with this mixture. Sew up both its openings and put it in a pan.

Wash and peel the potatoes. If they are big slice them. Add salt and pepper and arrange the potatoes around the duck. Pour the oil and the juice of the lemon over the duck and potatoes. Bake in a medium oven. During baking time baste the duck and the potatoes from time to time. When the food is done, remove the string that was used to sew up the bird. Cut the duck into portions and serve it garnished with potatoes on one side and the stuffing on the other.

5-6 SERVINGS

◇ 1 medium-sized duck

◇ 200 grams (7 oz) olive oil

◇ 2 spoonfuls butter

◇ ½ kilo (1 lb 2 oz) chestnuts

◇ 100 grams (3 ½ oz) almonds, blanched

◇ 100 grams (3 ½ oz) white raisins

◇ 1 kilo (2 lbs 4 oz) potatoes

◇ 1 lemon

◇ Salt-pepper

Kotópoulo me Trahaná

CHICKEN WITH «TRAHANA»

5 - 6 SERVINGS

◇ 1 ½ kilos (3 lbs 6 oz) chicken

◇ 1 kilo (2 lbs 4 oz) ripe tomatoes

◇ 1 soup-dish «trahana» (either the sweet or the sour variety, see p. 49)

◇ 1 large onion, grated

◇ 4 tablespoons butter

◇ Salt

Heat two tablespoons butter in a pot and sauté the onion over a medium fire. Wash the chicken and cut it into portions.
Add it to the sautéed onion.
Mash the tomatoes and add them to the pot. Place the chicken onto a platter, when it is done. Strain the broth from the pot. Return the stained broth to the pot and bring it to a boil. Add the «trahana» stirring constantly with a wooden spoon.
Just before the «trahana» is done, add the chicken to the pot and cook together for about 5 minutes. Finally, heat two tablespoons butter in a frying pan and pour it over the food. Serve hot.

Kotópoulo me Sáltsa Yaoúrti

CHICKEN WITH YOGHURT SAUCE

Clean the chicken, cut it into portions and boil it in plenty of salted water. Take the chicken out of the pot; drain the chicken, strain its broth, and keep them separately.
Mix 2 tablespoons yoghurt with some oil and coat the chicken pieces with this yoghurt-oil mix.
Place the chicken in a pan and grill it, until it turns golden brown. In the meantime, beat the remaining yoghurt with the egg and put it in a pot over a very low fire. When the yoghurt-egg mix begins to boil, add as much broth, as is necessary to create a thick sauce. Then add the mint, salt and pepper and a scalded tablespoon of butter.

Mix everything together. In another pot, boil salted water. Remove the pot from the fire and put the rice in it for 5 minutes to soak. Rinse and drain the rice.

Measure 3 parts of the remaining chicken broth to 1 part rice. Boil the broth in a pot and add the rice for 10 minutes. Heat the remaining butter and scald the rice with it. Serve the rice and the chicken with the sauce separately.

5 - 6 SERVINGS

◇ 1 ½ kilos (3 lbs 6 oz) chicken

◇ 1 kilo (2 lbs 4 oz) yoghurt

◇ 1 egg

◇ 3 tablespoons butter

◇ ½ kilo (1 lb 2 oz) rice

◇ Mint

◇ Olive oil

Game meats

- *Quails with Rice in Tomato Sauce*

- *Hare with Carrots and Mushrooms*

- *Wild Duck with Oranges*

Agriópapia me Portokália

WILD DUCK WITH ORANGES

Heat the butter in a pot. Over a medium fire, sauté the onions lightly and add the wild duck portions. Sauté for another 10 minutes stirring constantly. Pour in the liqueur and the orange juice, add the basil, salt, pepper, and some water. Let everything boil for about an hour and a half.

In the meantime, peel the oranges very well, cut them into round slices and place them on one side of the pot. Continue cooking for a further half an hour (approximately).

When there is very little sauce left in the pot, remove it from the fire and serve.

6 SERVINGS

- ◇ 1 wild duck, approximately 1 ½ kilos (3 lbs 6 oz), 6 portions
- ◇ 1 kilo (2 lbs 4 oz) oranges
- ◇ 1 teacup butter
- ◇ 2 onions, finely chopped
- ◇ 1 wine glass orange juice
- ◇ 1 wine glass orange liqueur
- ◇ 1 teaspoon basil
- ◇ Salt-pepper

Kounéli me Stafídes

RABBIT WITH RAISINS

4-5 SERVINGS

- ◇ 1 rabbit with its entrails
- ◇ 1 clove stick
- ◇ 1 lemon, cut into round slices
- ◇ 4-5 tablespoons tomato sauce
- ◇ 1 glass of wine
- ◇ 1 teacup white raisins
- ◇ ½ pepper
- ◇ Pinch of thyme
- ◇ 2-3 cloves garlic
- ◇ 2 onions, finely chopped
- ◇ 1 ½ teacups olive oil
- ◇ Salt-pepper

Cut the rabbit into portions and sauté them in a pot with oil; season with salt and pepper.

In a frying pan, sauté the liver of the rabbit in oil. Add the onions and the garlic, finely chopped. Empty the contents of the frying pan in the pot with the rabbit. Continue by adding the pepper (finely chopped), the thyme, the clove stick, the lemon slices, the tomato sauce and, finally, the raisins and the wine. Add the required amount of water and cook over a low fire.

The meal is ready, when there is only a small amount of tasty sauce left in the pot. Serve hot.

Agriokoúnelo me Karóta ke Manitária

HARE WITH CARROTS AND MUSHROOMS

6 SERVINGS

◇ 1 hare, 1 ½ kilos approximately (3 lbs 6 oz), 6 portions
◇ ½ kilo (1 lb 2 oz) carrots
◇ ½ kilo (1 lb 2 oz) mushrooms
◇ 1 teacup olive oil
◇ 1 wine glass red wine
◇ 1 clove garlic
◇ 1 ripe tomato, finely diced
◇ 2 onions, finely diced
◇ Salt-pepper

Heat the oil in a pot and lightly sauté the onions over a medium fire.

Next, add the portions of hare and sauté for 10 more minutes, until the meat is golden brown. Pour in the red wine; add the tomato, the garlic, the carrots (scraped and cut in round slices), the mushrooms, salt and pepper and let everything boil for about an hour and a half.

When there is only a little sauce left in the pot, the food will be ready. Serve hot.

Ortykia «Atzém» Piláfi

QUAILS WITH RICE IN TOMATO SAUCE

Heat the oil in a pot and sauté the onions lightly. Add the quails, washed and cleaned. Sauté the quails with the onions over a medium fire for about ten minutes stirring constantly.

Next, add the tomatoes, the garlic, the salt and pepper and some water.

Let everything cook for about an hour. Finally, add the rice (1 part rice to 2 parts water) and continue cooking for a further 15 minutes. Serve hot.

6 SERVINGS

◇ 12 quails (about 1 ½ kilos or 3 lbs 6 oz)
◇ ½ kilo (1 lb 2 oz) rice, washed and strained
◇ 1 teacup olive oil
◇ 2 onions, finely diced
◇ 2 ripe tomatoes, finely diced
◇ 1 clove garlic
◇ Salt-pepper

Pérdikes me Anginâres

PARTRIDGES WITH ARTICHOKES

6 SERVINGS

◇ 6 partridges

◇ 12 small-sized artichokes

◇ 2 spring onions, finely chopped

◇ 2 tomatoes, finely diced

◇ 2 tablespoons dill

◇ Some finely chopped parsley

◇ 1 lemon

◇ Olive oil

◇ Salt-pepper

Singe excess feathers from the birds. Heat the oil in a pot and sauté the onions lightly. Add the partridges which have been washed and cleaned well. Brown the birds for about 10 minutes while constantly stirring. Add the tomatoes, the salt, the pepper, and an adequate amount of water, and let the food cook for about 30 minutes.

In the meantime, prepare the artichokes by removing their tough outer leaves. With a sharp knife scoop all the «hairy inside» in the middle of the heart out and cut them vertically down the centre. Rub the prepared artichokes with the lemon, place them in water so that they will not turn black and let them stand for a while. When the artichokes are ready, add them to the pot with the partridges. Add the dill and the parsley and continue cooking for another half an hour. The partridges are served with the artichokes beside them.

Partridges with Artichokes ➤

Hare Ragout ➤

Wild Boar with Maize and Red Peppers ➤

Lagós Stifádo

HARE RAGOUT

Cut the hare into small pieces, wash well and drain. Heat the oil in a pot and add the pieces of hare.

Next, add the onions, which have been peeled but left whole, and let them sauté along with the hare for about 10 minutes.

Pour in the vinegar, add the tomatoes, the garlic, the rosemary, the bay leaf, the salt, the pepper and an adequate amount of water.

Let everything cook for about 2 hours. When there is only a little sauce left in the pot, the meal is ready. Serve hot as a second course.

Note: *this dish is rich. We recommend you to avoid having if for supper.*

6 SERVINGS

◇ 1 hare, 1 ½ kilos approximately (3 lbs 6 oz), 6 portions

◇ 1 kilo (2 lbs 4 oz) small, pickling sized, onions

◇ 1 teacup olive oil

◇ 1 teacup vinegar

◇ 2-3 ripe tomatoes, finely diced

◇ 2 cloves garlic

◇ 1 bay leaf

◇ 1 branch rosemary

◇ Salt

◇ Coarsely ground pepper

Agrióhiros me Kalambokákia ke Piperiés

WILD BOAR WITH MAIZE (INDIAN CORN) AND RED PEPPERS

Heat the oil in a pot and sauté the onions lightly over a medium fire. Then add the wild boar, cut into portions, and let it brown for about 10 minutes, constantly stirring. Pour in the red wine and add the tomatoes, the rosemary, salt and pepper, some water and let everything cook for about an hour. Next, add the maize and peppers and continue cooking for another hour, approximately; add a small amount of water, if needed. The meal is ready, when there is only a small amount of broth left in the pot.

Note: *this is a rich dish. Therefore, avoid having it for supper.*

6 SERVINGS

- ◇ 1 wild boar, 1 ½ kilos (3 lbs 6 oz) approx.
- ◇ 500 grams (1 lb 2 oz) small-sized maize (Indian corn)
- ◇ 500 grams (1 lb 2 oz) red peppers, coarsely cut
- ◇ 2 onions, finely diced
- ◇ 2-3 ripe tomatoes, diced
- ◇ 1 small branch rosemary
- ◇ Pepper corns
- ◇ 1 glass red wine
- ◇ Olive oil
- ◇ Salt

Trygónia Krassáta

TURTLEDOVES IN WINE SAUCE

Clean the turtledoves well, wash and drain them. Season them with salt and pepper and coat them with oil. Put the seasoned birds in the refrigerator for two hours.

Heat the remaining oil in a pot and, when it is scalding hot, sauté the turtledoves in it.

Pour in the wine and cover the pot.

Next, add the cinnamon and the allspice and 2 glasses warm water. When the birds are half done, add the tomatoes and cook, until most liquids are absorbed and the birds are left with only a small amount of tasty sauce. Serve hot with fried potatoes or pilaf.

4-5 SERVINGS

- ◇ 8 turtledoves
- ◇ ½ kilo (1 lb 2 oz) tomatoes, finely diced
- ◇ 1 teacup white wine
- ◇ 1 teacup olive oil
- ◇ Cinnamon stick
- ◇ Allspice
- ◇ Salt-pepper

Bekátses me Ryzi

WOODCOCKS WITH RICE

4 SERVINGS

◇ 2 large woodcocks
◇ ½ teacup butter
◇ ½ teacup brandy
◇ 1 tablespoon flour
◇ 1 teacup fresh tomato, mashed
◇ ½ tablespoon vinegar
◇ ½ kilo (1 lb 2 oz) rice for pilaf, washed and strained
◇ Mint
◇ Salt-pepper

Clean the woodcocks removing the entrails. Wash them both inside and out and drain.

Heat the butter in a pot and sauté the birds.

Season with salt and pepper. Scald the brandy in a small saucepan and pour it scalding hot into the pot with the woodcocks.

Add two tablespoons of water and cook for about 30 minutes.

Separately cook the rice. Scald it with a small amount of butter and shape it onto a platter.

Cut the woodcocks in half and lay them on the platter over the rice.

Into the pot with the leftover sauce (from the birds), stir in the flour. While continuing to stir, add the tomato, the vinegar, the mint and a little bit salt.

Cook for a few minutes. Pour the sauce over the woodcocks and rice. Serve immediately.

Pitsoúnia Kokinistá

PIGEONS IN TOMATO SAUCE

Singe excess feathers from the pigeons, wash them and dry them well; season with salt and pepper. Heat the butter in a pot and sauté the birds whole. Pour in the wine and place the peeled tomatoes around the birds.

Add the required amount of water and simmer over a low fire. When the birds are done, remove them from the pot and place them in the centre of a platter. Take care to cook the tomatoes properly (do not over or undercook) and try to take them out whole. Fry the sliced bread in butter and arrange the slices on the platter around the birds. Place a tomato on each slice of bread and pour the sauce over the birds. Serve immediately.

4 SERVINGS

◇ 2 whole pigeons
◇ 3-4 tablespoons butter
◇ 1 teacup white wine
◇ 500 grams (1 lb 2 oz) small, ripe tomatoes, peeled
◇ Slices of bread
◇ Salt-pepper

Fish & Seafood

- *Fried Sole Fish*
- *Squid with Rice and Red Peppers*
- *Boiled Lobster with Vegetables*
- *Fish in Tomato Sauce*

Astakós Vrastós me Hortariká

BOILED LOBSTER WITH VEGETABLES

Pour enough water into a pot so as to cover the lobster. Add the onions, the carrots, the celery, the bay leaf, the vinegar, the salt and pepper and cook for about 20 minutes.

Next, carefully place the lobster in the pot and continue cooking for another 25-30 minutes. Remove the lobster and the vegetables from the pot and place them on a platter. When the lobster is cold enough, cut it in two, lengthwise with a sharp knife. Serve the lobster in portions with the boiled vegetables (and asparagus, mushrooms, potatoes, etc., if desired).

5-6 SERVINGS

- 1 lobster, about 1 ½ kilos (3 lbs 6 oz)
- 2-3 carrots, coarsely cut
- 1-2 onions, coarsely diced
- Small amount of celery
- 1 bay leaf
- 1 wine glass vinegar
- 2 teaspoons pepper corns
- Salt

Glósses Tiganités

FRIED SOLE FISH

Wash and clean the sole as follows:

Salt the edge of the tail and rub it well with you fingers, until you grip the skin. Steadily pull the skin back, until it comes off. Repeat this process on the other side. With a scissor remove the fins and the head of the fish and place the sole in a pan. Pour the lemon juice over the fish and season with salt and pepper.

Drain the fish and coat them with flour.

Beat the eggs with a small amount of water and spread this mixture over the fish. Heat the butter in a frying pan, until it melts. Fry the fish for about 10 minutes over a medium fire. Serve either with mayonnaise or a sauce with herbs (both recipes on p. 54-55).

5-6 SERVINGS

- 6 sole fish (Soleidae) of medium size
- 1 ½ teacups butter
- 2 eggs
- The juice of one lemon
- 1 teacup flour
- Salt-pepper

Kalamarákia me Ryzi ke Kókini Piperiá

SQUID WITH RICE AND RED PEPPERS

5 - 6 SERVINGS

◇ 1 kilo (2 lbs 4 oz) squid

◇ ½ kilo (1 lb 2 oz) rice, washed and strained

◇ 2-3 onions, medium sized, finely diced

◇ 2-3 red peppers, finely chopped

◇ 1 tablespoon parsley, finely chopped

◇ 1 teacup olive oil

◇ Salt-pepper

Prepare the squid as follows: Remove the tentacles, the ink sacks and the fine inner bone. Cut the squid in two and wash them well to remove all the sand, they may contain.

In a pot, sauté the onions in the oil, until they are golden. Add the squid and the peppers and let them sauté for another five minutes. Next, add some water and let it boil for about 15 minutes.

Continue by adding the rice and the parsley. Allow everything to cook for another 15 minutes over a medium fire. Serve hot as a main dish.

Psári Plakí

FISH CASSEROLE

Wash the slices of fish, place them in a pot and pour the lemon juice over them.

5 - 6 SERVINGS

◇ 6 medium-sized slices of fish, e.g. grouper (Epinephelus Aeneas or E. Caninus)

◇ 3-4 onions, cut in slices

◇ 2-3 ripe tomatoes, finely diced

◇ 1 ½ teacups olive oil

◇ The juice of one lemon

◇ ½ teacup parsley, finely chopped

◇ Salt-pepper

Season with salt and pepper and let them stand for about an hour. Heat the oil in a pot and lightly sauté the onions in it. Add the tomatoes, the parsley, salt and pepper and allow these to cook for about 20 minutes.

Finally, carefully place the slices of fish in the pot. Cover the pot and let it cook for another 15 minutes. Serve as a first course.

Galéos Tiganitós

FRIED HOUND SHARK

Wash and clean the fish. Cut it into slices. Pour the lemon juice over the shark, season it with salt and pepper and let it stand (in a pan) for about an hour. Place plenty of oil in a frying pan and heat it until boiling. Flour the fish slices. Beat two eggs with a small amount of water and coat the fish with this mixture. Drain the fish and fry each piece for about 10-15 minutes. Serve hot accompanied by garlic sauce or mayonnaise.

5-6 SERVINGS
◇ 1 ½ kilos (3 lbs 6 oz) hound shark (scyliorhinus)
◇ 2 eggs
◇ The juice of one lemon
◇ Oil for frying
◇ Salt-pepper

Fried Hound Shark ➤

Shrimps with Spinach and Feta Cheese ➤

Garídes me Spanáki ke Féta

SHRIMPS WITH SPINACH AND FETA CHEESE

In a pot, heat the oil and sauté the onions and dill lightly. Wash the spinach, shred it roughly and add it to the pot with the sautéed onions. Allow these to boil over a medium fire for about 25 minutes and add the shrimps. Cook for another 5 minutes. Carefully place the vegetables and shrimps in a pan, sprinkle over with the Feta that has been broken into large bits, and season to taste. Bake in a medium oven for 10 minutes. Serve hot.

5-6 SERVINGS
◇ 1 kilo (2 lbs 4 oz) shrimps
◇ ½ kilo (1 lb 2 oz) spinach
◇ 2-3 spring onions, sliced
◇ 300 grams (11 oz) Feta cheese
◇ ½ teacup dill, finely chopped
◇ 1 teacup olive oil
◇ Salt-pepper

Bourdéto Kérkyras

FISH IN TOMATO SAUCE

Clean and wash the fish, season with salt and keep them aside.

Prepare the sauce as follows:

In a pot, sauté the onions in oil, until they look golden brown. Add the tomatoes, peeled and finely diced, salt and red pepper, a little water, if necessary, and let the sauce boil,

5 - 6 SERVINGS
◇ Various fish, e.g. scorpion fish, etc.
◇ ½ kilo (1 lb 2 oz) onions, finely chopped
◇ 1 kilo ripe tomatoes
◇ 1 ½ teacups olive oil
◇ 1 tablespoon red pepper
◇ Salt

until it thickens up. Finally, carefully place the fish in the pot and let everything cook over a medium fire for about 15 minutes.

Krokétes Bakaliárou

SALTED COD CROQUETTES

5 - 6 SERVINGS
◇ 500 grams (1 lb 2 oz) salted, frozen or fresh cod fish
◇ 500 grams (1 lb 2 oz) potatoes
◇ 3 eggs
◇ 1 tablespoon olive oil
◇ 50 grams (2 oz) butter
◇ 1 teacup toasted breadcrumbs
◇ Oil for frying
◇ Salt-pepper

In case that salted cod is used, cut it into portions and let it soak for 24 hours. Wash the potatoes and boil them in salted water. Put the codfish in a pot with plenty of water and boil for two minutes. Cover the pot and let it stand for a while. Remove the codfish from the pot, skin and bone it and cut into very small pieces.

Peel the cooked potatoes. Mash them and mix them with the codfish, 2 eggs yolks, the oil, salt and pepper with a wooden spoon. Let the mixture cool down on its own.

Beat the third egg separately, along with the whites of the other two eggs. Shape the codfish mixture into rectangular croquettes. Dip into the beaten eggs, then coat them with the crumbs and finally fry them in plenty of oil on both sides, until they look golden brown.

Héli me Spanáki sto Foúrno

BAKED EEL WITH SPINACH

Cut the eel into slices. Wash the spinach very well and drain it. Line a pan with spinach. Over the spinach make a layer of eel slices. Make a spinach layer over the eel layer and then another eel layer. Finally, on top, make a layer of spinach.

Add the oil, salt and pepper and little water and bake in the oven.

Test with a fork to see if the food is done. Serve hot.

5 - 6 SERVINGS
◇ 1 eel (approx. 1 ½ kilos or 3 lbs 6 oz)
◇ 1 kilo (2 lbs 4 oz) spinach
◇ 250 grams (9 oz) olive oil
◇ Salt
◇ Red pepper

Savóre Mykónou

FRIED FISH WITH A WINE VINEGAR SAUCE

5 - 6 SERVINGS
◇ 1 kilo (2 lbs 4 oz) fish, e.g. saddled breams, (Oblada Melanura) etc.
◇ ½ teacup wine vinegar
◇ ½ teacup water
◇ 1 wine glass olive oil
◇ A branch of rosemary
◇ 1 tablespoon flour
◇ Salt-black pepper

Prepare the fish accordingly, wash and season with salt. Flour the fish lightly and fry in oil in a frying pan, once the oil is quite hot. Take the fish out, as soon as they become pale golden on both sides, and keep them aside.

Prepare the sauce as follows:
Strain the contents of the frying pan, being careful not to include any burnt sediments, pour the strained oil in a saucepan and heat up. Add the flour and stir with a wooden spatula in order to become a mixture on medium heat. When this mix turns slightly brown, add the vinegar, the rosemary, the water, season to taste and let it cook, until the sauce thickens up. Finally, add the fried fish back into this sauce and simmer for about 5 minutes. Serve hot.

Vegetable Dishes

- *Okra cooked in oil*
- *Tomatoes and Peppers Stuffed with Rice*
- *Green Peas with Spring Onions*
- *Stewed Green Beans and Potatoes*

Domátes ke Piperiés Yemistés

TOMATOES AND PEPPERS STUFFED WITH RICE

5 - 6 SERVINGS

- ◇ 12 medium sized, ripe tomatoes
- ◇ 6 green peppers
- ◇ 2-3 onions, finely chopped
- ◇ 1 ½ teacups olive oil
- ◇ 3 tablespoons finely chopped parsley
- ◇ 1 tablespoon sugar
- ◇ 1 teaspoon mint
- ◇ ½ kilo (1 lb 2 oz) rice
- ◇ Salt-pepper

Wash the tomatoes and peppers. Using a sharp knife, cut a thin, round slice off the top, stem end of each one and keep aside to use them later as a lid-like cover. With a teaspoon remove the seeds from the peppers and scoop the tomato pulp out. Place the tomato pulp in a bowl and shred it finely. Arrange the hollowed out tomatoes and peppers in a baking dish, season with salt and pepper and sprinkle a little sugar in each tomato.

In a pot, sauté the onions in the oil on a medium fire. When slightly golden, add the rice, washed and strained, the parsley, the mint, the reserved, shredded tomato pulp, salt, pepper, a little water and let these cook for 10 minutes.

Next, fill the tomatoes and peppers, only three-quarters full, with the prepared stuffing. Cover them with the reserved round tops and bake them in a medium oven for about 45 minutes.

Note: *You may also insert some slices of potatoes between the tomatoes and peppers.*
You might also pour the juice of 2 tomatoes mixed with 1 teacup olive oil, over the stuffed vegetables. This way this dish will be more juicy.

Fassolákia me Patátes Yahní

STEWED GREEN BEANS AND POTATOES

5 - 6 SERVINGS

◇ 1 kilo (2 lbs 4oz) green beans

◇ 2 medium sized potatoes

◇ 3-4 ripe tomatoes, finely chopped

◇ 2 garlic cloves

◇ 2 tablespoons, finely chopped parsley

◇ 2-3 onions, finely chopped

◇ 1 ½ teacups olive oil

◇ Salt-pepper

Using a sharp knife, top and tail the green beans, cut off their edges and slice them it two, lengthwise. Sauté the onions and garlic cloves in the oil, in a pot, until transparent. Wash and strain the beans. Add them to the pot and let them sauté for five minutes, stirring constantly.

Then add the potatoes, (peeled and sliced), the tomatoes, the parsley, salt and pepper, the required amount of water and let everything cook for about half an hour on medium heat.

Serve either hot or cold with Feta or any other kind of cheese.

Arakás (Bizélia) me Kremydákia

GREEN PEAS WITH SPRING ONIONS

In a pot, sauté the onions in the oil, until transparent. Add the peas (cleaned and washed, in case they are fresh), the dill, salt, pepper, and some water and let these boil on medium heat for about 25 minutes.

5 - 6 SERVINGS

◇ 1 kilo (2 lbs 3 oz) green peas

◇ 200 grams (7oz) small onions

◇ 2-3 spring onions

◇ 2 tablespoons finely chopped dill

◇ 1 ½ teacups olive oil

◇ Salt-pepper

Serve either warm or cold as a first course. This dish also accompanies grilled or sautéed meat.

Melitzánes Fétes Yahní me Skórdo

AUBERGINE SLICES IN TOMATO AND GARLIC SAUCE

Remove the stem ends of the aubergines (eggplants) and cut them into slices. Place the slices in salted water for about 1 hour. Drain and fry them in plenty of oil. Place them in a cooking pan and add the onions, the garlic, the tomatoes, the sugar, salt, pepper and some water and let them boil on medium heat for 20-25 minutes.

Serve warm or cold with Feta cheese.

5-6 SERVINGS
- 4-5 aubergines (eggplants)
- 2-3 onions, finely chopped
- 5-6 garlic cloves, sliced
- 4-5 ripe tomatoes, finely chopped
- 2 teacups oil for frying
- 1 tablespoon sugar
- Salt-pepper

Aubergine Slices in Tomato and Garlic Sauce ➤

Baked Vegetables with Tomato Sauce ➤

Hortariká Briám

BAKED VEGETABLES WITH TOMATO SAUCE

Wash the vegetables; remove the stem ends of the courgettes, the aubergines and the peppers and peel the potatoes and onions. Then cut them into thick slices and place them in a baking or a pyrex dish. Add the tomatoes, the parsley, the mint, the oil, salt and pepper and mix them well. Add a little warm water and bake in a medium oven for about 90 minutes.

Serve warm a first course with Feta cheese.

5-6 SERVINGS
- 1 kilo (2 lbs 4 oz) potatoes
- 2-3 courgettes, medium sized
- 2 aubergines, medium sized
- 3-4 medium sized tomatoes, chopped
- 2-3 green peppers
- 2 teacups olive oil
- 2-3 onions
- 1 teaspoon mint, finely chopped
- Some parsley, chopped
- Salt-pepper

Anginátes me Patátes ke Karóta

ARTICHOKES WITH POTATOES AND CARROTS

5 - 6 SERVINGS

◇ 6 large artichokes
◇ 1 kilo (2 lbs 4 oz) carrots, scraped
◇ 1 kilo (2 lbs 4 oz) potatoes
◇ 1 teacup olive oil
◇ 2 spring onions, finely chopped
◇ Dill, finely chopped
◇ Some lettuce leaves
◇ 3 lemons
◇ Salt-pepper

Prepare the artichokes as described on p. 106, and rub them with a lemon cup. Quarter the artichokes and drop them in a bowl of water containing the juice of one lemon and a lemon cup.

In a pot, heat the oil and sauté the onions and the dill lightly. Add the artichokes stems, the potatoes (peeled and sliced, lengthwise), the carrots and the required amount of water. When these vegetables are half-cooked, add the artichokes and simmer until all the water (except the oil) is gone.

Serve garnished with the lettuce leaves.

Brókola Yahnistá

STEWED BROCCOLI

Clean and wash the broccoli, cut it into small pieces and drain.

Heat half the oil in a pot and sauté the garlic. Place the broccoli pieces in the pot (upright), add salt and pepper, the carrots (cut into round slices), the finely chopped tomatoes, the remaining oil and the required amount of water.

Cover the pot, lower the fire and simmer, until all the water is gone and the broccoli is left in its sauce. Serve hot.

5 - 6 SERVINGS

◇ 1 ½ kilos (3 lbs 6 oz) broccoli
◇ 2-3 carrots
◇ 4-5 cloves garlic
◇ 4-5 ripe tomatoes, finely chopped
◇ 1 teacup olive oil
◇ Salt-pepper

AnginJres me KoukiJ

ARTICHOKES WITH BROAD BEANS

5 - 6 SERVINGS

◇ 2 kilos (4 lbs 8 oz) broad beans

◇ 10 artichokes

◇ 2 gloves garlic

◇ 3-4 ripe tomatoes, chopped

◇ ½ kilo (1 lb 2 oz) olive oil

◇ ½ teaspoon pepper

◇ Salt

◇ The juice of 2 lemons

◇ Some fennel

Prepare the artichokes, as described on (p. 106), rub them with a lemon cup and let them stand in water for a while.

Clean the broad beans. Finely chop the garlic and the fennel and mix them in a bowl with the tomatoes, the salt and pepper, and half the oil.

Stuff the artichokes (which have been hollowed) with the mix from the bowl.

Place the artichokes upright in a pot and drop the beans over them. Pour in the remaining oil.

Add the required amount of water and cook over a low fire without stirring. Cook until all liquids are absorbed and only the oil is left. Serve hot and accompany with Feta cheese.

Prássa Yahní

STEWED LEEKS

4 - 5 SERVINGS

◇ 1 kilo (2 lbs 4 oz) leeks

◇ 5 carrots, finely chopped

◇ Plenty of celery

◇ 1 onion

◇ 1 kilo (2 lbs 4 oz) ripe tomatoes, chopped

◇ 1 bay leaf

◇ A stick of cinnamon

◇ A liqueur glass of vinegar

◇ 2 teacups olive oil

◇ Salt-pepper

Top and tail the leeks. Discard the coarse outer leaves and wash them well. Slice them in 2-cm (3/4-inch) rings and place them in a pot.

Let them simmer on low heat without adding any water. When the leeks begin to wilt, add the finely chopped carrots, the celery, the onion, the tomatoes, the oil, the salt, the bay leaf, the cinnamon, the pepper, and the required amount of water. Cover the pot and cook over a low fire, until the water is gone and the vegetables are left in their sauce.

Just before cooking is done, add the vinegar.

Melitzánes Imambaildí

BAKED AUBERGINES STUFFED WITH TOMATO SAUCE

5 - 6 SERVINGS

◇ 6 aubergines, medium-sized
◇ 4-5 onions, cut in round slices
◇ 2-3 ripe tomatoes, skinned and finely chopped
◇ 2 tomatoes, cut into slices
◇ 3 tablespoons finely chopped parsley
◇ 3-4 garlic cloves, sliced
◇ 2 teacups olive oil
◇ 2 teaspoons sugar
◇ Salt-pepper

Remove the stem ends of the aubergines. Slice them in half, lengthwise. Drop them in a pot with salted water for about 1 hour to remove their bitter juices. Strain them well and fry them in plenty of oil over a medium fire. Next, arrange the fried aubergines in a baking dish.

Using a teaspoon scoop half their pulp out; place the pulp in a bowl and keep it aside. In a saucepan, sauté the onions in oil, adding the chopped tomatoes, the garlic, the reserved pulp, the parsley, the sugar, salt and pepper. Let these cook for about 20 minutes over a medium fire. Fill the aubergines with the prepared stuffing, cover each stuffed aubergine with a tomato slice and bake in a medium oven for about 45 minutes.

Kolokythákia Avgolémono

COURGETTES (ZUCCHINIS) IN EGG AND LEMON SAUCE

5 - 6 SERVINGS

◇ 12 medium-sized courgettes (zucchinis)

◇ 3 onions, finely chopped

◇ 2 teacups long-grain rice, washed and strained

◇ 1 teacup olive oil

◇ 2 tablespoons parsley

◇ 1 tablespoon mint

◇ 2 eggs

◇ The juice of 1 lemon

◇ Salt-pepper

Wash the courgettes (zucchinis). Using a teaspoon scoop their middle fleshy part out, being careful not to damage their skin. Shred the courgette pulp finely, place it in a bowl and keep it aside. In a pot, sauté the onions in the oil on medium heat. Add the shredded courgette pulp, the rice, the parsley, the mint, a little water, salt and pepper. Let them cook for 10 minutes on a medium fire. Take off the heat. Fill the hollowed courgettes with the prepared stuffing. Place them in a large saucepan, add a small amount of water and cook over a medium fire for about 35-40 minutes.

Prepare the egg and lemon sauce as follows:

In a bowl, beat the egg whites with an egg-beater; add the egg yolks, beating all the time. Gradually add the lemon juice and some broth from the saucepan with the stuffed courgettes. Remove the saucepan from the fire. Pour the egg and lemon sauce over the courgettes shaking the saucepan a few times, so that the sauce spreads everywhere. Serve warm.

Lahanóryzo

CABBAGE RICE

5 - 6 SERVINGS

- ◇ 1 ½ teacups rice, washed and strained
- ◇ 1 medium-sized cabbage
- ◇ 1 onion
- ◇ 2 tablespoons butter
- ◇ Pinch of parsley
- ◇ 1 tablespoon tomato paste
- ◇ Salt-pepper
- ◇ Grated cheese (optional)

Wash the cabbage well and shred finely. Heat the butter in a pot and sauté the onion until transparent. Add the shredded cabbage and continue to sauté. Dilute the tomato paste in a glass of water and pour it into the pot with the cabbage stirring constantly. Finally add a small amount of water.

When the cabbage is almost done, add the parsley, the rice and the salt.

Continue to cook until there is only a little sauce left in the pot. Serve hot with dashes of lemon juice. Sprinkle with grated cheese, if it is preferred.

Bámies Laderés

OKRA (LADY'S FINGERS) COOKED IN OIL

Trim off the okra stems and place them in a bowl with salt, water and 1 teacup of vinegar. Leave them for 1 hour. Rinse them thoroughly 2-3 times with plenty of water. Leave them to strain. Sauté the onions and garlic in the oil until lightly brown. Add the okra and keep turning for 5 minutes. Add the finely chopped tomatoes, salt, pepper, some water and let them boil in medium heat for about 1½ hour. Serve warm or cold.

5 - 6 SERVINGS

- ◇ 1 kilo (2 lbs 3 oz) okra
- ◇ 2-3 ripe tomatoes, finely chopped
- ◇ 2-3 onions, finely chopped
- ◇ 2 garlic cloves, finely chopped
- ◇ 1 ½ teacups olive oil
- ◇ 1 teacup vinegar
- ◇ Salt-pepper
- ◇ 2 tablespoons of finely chopped parsley

Spanáki sto Foúrno

SPINACH IN THE OVEN

5 - 6 SERVINGS

◇ 1 ½ kilos (3 lbs 6 oz) spinach

◇ 400 grams (14 oz) Kefalotyri cheese, grated

◇ 7 eggs

◇ 7 tablespoons toasted breadcrumbs

◇ 5 potatoes, boiled

◇ Butter

◇ Olive oil

◇ Salt-pepper

Clean and wash the spinach. Shred it and rub in some salt. Wash the spinach again, squeeze the excess moisture and put it in bowl. Add 250 grams (9 oz) Kefalotyri cheese, the crumbs, some oil and 5 eggs. Mix well. Oil a pan and put it in the oven. When the oil is very hot, line the pan with the mix you have prepared. Sprinkle over with some grated Kefalotyri cheese and make openings, the size of small lemons, in the spinach mix. In a bowl, mash the boiled potatoes. Mix in the two eggs, the remaining grated cheese, some butter, and salt and pepper. Mix the mashed potatoes, eggs and cheese well and using a teaspoon place quantities of this mixture into the openings in the spinach layer. Spread with a little bit of oil and butter and bake in a medium oven.

Patátes Yemistés

STUFFED POTATOES

Bake the potatoes in a low oven, until they can be easily pierced by a fork. Remove the potatoes from the oven and cut off their tops. With a spoon scoop out most of their pulp. Do not discard the pulp but put it in a bowl, season with salt and pepper and mash. Stuff the hollowed potatoes with their mashed pulp leaving openings at the tops.

6 SERVINGS

◇ 6 large, round potatoes

◇ 6 eggs

◇ Grated cheese

◇ Some bread (crusts removed)

◇ Butter

◇ Salt-pepper

Break the eggs into the potato openings taking care not to break the yolks. Sprinkle with grated cheese, season with salt and pepper and cover with bread. Put the potatoes back into the oven. When the grated cheese browns, the potatoes are ready. Serve hot.

Desserts

- *Plaited Breads*
- *Short bread Cookies*
- *Sweet «Pleats»*
- *Baked Apples Stuffed with Walnuts and Raisins*
- *Honey Puffs*

Míla Psitá me Karýdia

BAKED APPLES STUFFED WITH WALNUTS AND RAISINS

Wash the apples. Remove their cores as well as some of their pulp. In a bowl, mix the walnuts, the raisins, the sugar and the brandy.

Place the apples in a pan and stuff them with the mix you have prepared. Sprinkle them with the cinnamon and bake them in a medium oven for about 45 minutes.

Remove the apples from the oven, let them cool and serve them with their own syrup or with whipped cream and cherries.

6 SERVINGS
- ◇ 6 large, round apples
- ◇ 150 grams (5 ½ oz) walnuts, pounded into crumbs
- ◇ 150 grams (5 ½ oz) raisins
- ◇ 1 tablespoon cinnamon
- ◇ 100 grams (3 ½ oz) sugar
- ◇ 1 small glass brandy

Tsourékia

PLAITED BREADS

Dissolve the yeast in the lukewarm water. Add a teacup of flour and beat the mix by hand, until it is smooth. Cover the yeast mix with a towel and place it in a warm place to rise. Slightly heat the milk, the sugar, the butter and the orange rind and place them in a bowl. Add the yeast, the eggs, beaten, and the flour, stirring constantly. Make sure the dough is neither too soft nor too tough. Cover this dough with a towel and let it stand in a warm place for about an hour and a half. When the dough has doubled in size, knead it again by hand and shape plaited breads.

Traditional Easter Breads
- ◇ 1 kilo (2 lbs 4 oz) flour
- ◇ 1 teacup butter
- ◇ 2 tablespoons grated orange rind
- ◇ 6 eggs
- ◇ 1 ½ teacups sugar
- ◇ ½ teacup milk
- ◇ 2 tablespoons yeast
- ◇ ½ teacup lukewarm water

Brush the breads with 2-3 beaten egg yolks and bake them in a medium oven for about 30-35 minutes.

Loukoumádes

HONEY PUFFS

◇ ½ kilo (1 lb 2 oz) flour

◇ 2 teaspoons yeast

◇ 1 teaspoon salt

◇ 2 teaspoons ground cinnamon

◇ Oil for frying

SYRUP

◇ 2 teacups honey

◇ 1 teacup sugar

◇ Stick of cinnamon

◇ 2 teacups water

Dissolve the yeast in lukewarm water. Put the flour and the salt in a bowl and gradually add the dissolved yeast mixing by hand. Next, gradually add some lukewarm water until you have a paste that is neither too fluid nor too thick. Cover the bowl with a towel and let it stand in warm water for about an hour. When the batter doubles in size and forms «bubbles», heat plenty of oil in a pot, until it is scalding hot. Drop teaspoonfuls of the batter into the hot oil. Allow the honey puffs to turn golden brown. Remove the honey puffs from the oil with a slotted spoon and place them onto a platter. In the meantime, prepare the syrup as follows:

In a pot, boil the honey, the sugar, the water and the cinnamon stick for 10 minutes. Pour the syrup over the honey puffs and sprinkle with cinnamon. Serve hot.

Kourambiédes

SHORT BREAD COOKIES (OR BISCUITS)

Let the butter soften and cream it for 15 minutes, until it begins to turn white. Add the egg yolks, the baking soda, the baking powder, the almonds, the brandy, and, finally, gradually add the flour, until you have a dough that is neither too soft nor too tough. Let the dough stand for an hour in a warm place covered by a towel. Next, with small amounts of dough shape round, rectangular or crescent cookies. Arrange them on a buttered pan and bake in a medium oven for 15-20 minutes. After removing the «kourambiedes» from the oven, sprinkle them with rose water. Finally, sift plenty of icing sugar over them.

Traditional Christmas Biscuits

◇ 2 teacups butter

◇ 2 egg yolks

◇ 3 teacups flour

◇ 1 teacup icing (confectioner's) sugar

◇ 1 teaspoon baking powder

◇ ½ teacup brandy

◇ ½ teaspoon baking soda

◇ 1 teacup almonds, chopped and roasted

◇ Some rose water

Sámali

SEMOLINA CAKE STEEPED IN SYRUP

Beat the butter and the sugar together; add the eggs and continue beating, until frothy. Next add the semolina, the almonds and the cinnamon. Mix well, until the mixture is not lumpy. Spread the mixture evenly in a buttered pan and bake in a medium oven for 30 minutes. Remove the cake from the oven and cut it into square shaped pieces, while it is still in the pan. In the meantime prepare the syrup as follows:

In a pot, boil the sugar, the water, and the juice of ½ a lemon for 10 minutes. Pour the syrup, scalding hot, over the cake, while the cake is still lukewarm.

◇ 2 teacups fine semolina
◇ 2 "teacups sugar
◇ 8 eggs
◇ 1 teacup butter
◇ 1 tablespoon cinnamon
◇ 1 teacup almonds, blanched and chopped

SYRUP
◇ 3 teacups sugar
◇ 3 teacups water
◇ ½ lemon

Semolina Cake Steeped in Syrup ➤

Almond Cookies ➤

Amygdalotá

ALMOND COOKIES (OR BISCUITS)

Beat the egg whites to a stiff meringue and gradually add the sugar and the almond crumbs. Mix the ingredients well and make with the batter round shapes. Stick almond slices on the surface of each cookie. Line a pan with waxed paper and place the cookies on it. Bake in a medium oven for about 15 minutes.

◇ 12 egg whites
◇ 300 grams (11 oz) icing (confectioner's) sugar
◇ 1 ½ kilos (3 lbs 6 oz) almonds, blanched and pounded into crumbs
◇ Waxed paper

Note: *The oven must have been pre-heated, before the pan is placed in it.*

Halvás

KIND OF PUDDING
WITH WALNUTS AND SYRUP

Heat the oil in a frying pan. Gradually, add the flour and the cinnamon stirring constantly, until the semolina looks dark brown. In the meantime, prepare the syrup by boiling the water and the sugar for about 10 minutes. Pour the syrup, scalding hot over the «halva» and stir constantly, until the mixture thickens up. Remove the frying pan from fire. When the «halva» cools down a little, place it in small containers such as muffin tins for it to acquire a nice shape. Serve onto a platter, sprinkled with walnuts.

◇ 1 teacup olive oil or butter
◇ 2 teacups not fine semolina
◇ 1 tablespoon cinnamon
◇ Chopped walnuts

SYRUP
◇ 3 teacups water
◇ 2 ½ teacups sugar

Díples

SWEET «PLEATS»

Beat the eggs in the mixer for 5 minutes. Add the ouzo, the baking soda (or baking powder), the lemon juice and the flour. Remove from the mixer and knead by hand until you have a tough dough. Cover the dough and let it stand for two hours. With a rolling pin roll the dough out into very thin leaves. Cut the leaves into square shapes. Press the edges of the squares together with your fingers so as to form bows (as on p. 197).
Heat the oil in a frying pan and fry the «pleats» on both sides, until they are golden brown. Place the sweet pleats on a tray and prepare the syrup as follows:
In a pot, place the sugar, the honey, the water and the cinnamon and boil for 15 minutes. Pour the syrup over the pleats and sprinkle with walnuts and cinnamon. Serve cold.

◇ 8 eggs
◇ 1 kilo (2 lbs 4 oz) flour
◇ 1 wine glass ouzo
◇ 1 teaspoon baking soda or baking powder
◇ Juice of half a lemon
◇ 250 grams (9 oz) walnut crumbs
◇ 2 teaspoons cinnamon crumbs
◇ 2 teaspoons cinnamon powder
◇ Refined oil for frying

SYRUP
◇ 2 teacups sugar
◇ 1 teacup honey
◇ 2 glasses water
◇ A stick of cinnamon

Baklavás me Amýgdala

«FYLLO» PASTRY STUFFED WITH HEAVILY SPICED ALMONDS

◇ ½ kilo (1 lb 2 oz) «fyllo» pastry

◇ 2 teacups almonds, pounded into crumbs

◇ 1 ½ teacups butter

◇ ½ teacup sugar

◇ 1 tablespoon cinnamon

SYRUP

◇ 3 teacups sugar

◇ 1 teacup honey

◇ 2 teacups water

◇ Cinnamon stick

◇ 1 tablespoon clove sticks

In a bowl, mix the pounded almonds, the sugar and the cinnamon. Butter a small pan and lay a few sheets of «fyllo» pastry onto it brushing each one with butter. Next, spread a small amount of the almond mix over the «fyllo» layer. Continue by making successive layers of «fyllo» and almond mix of about equal thickness. Finish with a thicker layer of «fyllo» sheets (6-8 sheets) brushing each sheet with butter. With a sharp knife cut the «baklava» into diamond-shaped pieces. Sprinkle with water and bake in a medium oven for about an hour.

In the meantime, prepare the syrup as follows: In a pot, place the water, the honey, the sugar, and the spices and boil them oven a strong fire for about 15 minutes.

When the «baklava» is ready, remove it from the oven and let it cool. Pour the boiling syrup over it. Cut out the pieces that were marked before baking.

Note: *you may make smaller pieces of baklava in the same way, as well.*

Yaourtópita

YOGHURT CAKE

Beat butter and sugar together until fluffy and then add the eggs, one-by-one, beating constantly. Next, mix in the yoghurt and sift the flour and baking powder. Continue to beat until the batter is fluid. Place the mixture in a buttered pan and bake in a medium oven for about an hour.

◇ 2 teacups flour

◇ 2 teacups sugar

◇ 4 eggs

◇ 300 grams (11 oz) yoghurt (made from cow's milk)

◇ 250 grams (9 oz) butter

◇ Baking powder

Kataífi me Karýdia

FINELY SHREDDED PASTRY ROLL FILLED WITH WALNUTS AND STEEPED IN SYRUP

- ◇ ½ kilo (1 lb 2 oz) pastry sheet for «kataifi», i.e. finely shredded pastry
- ◇ 250 grams (9 oz) walnuts, finely chopped
- ◇ 100 grams (3 ½ oz) sugar
- ◇ 1 teaspoon ground cinnamon
- ◇ 1 ½ teacups butter

SYRUP
- ◇ 3 teacups sugar
- ◇ 2 teacups water
- ◇ The rind of one lemon
- ◇ The juice of one lemon

In a bowl, mix the walnuts, the sugar and the cinnamon. Next, take a small amount of «kataifi» pastry and spread it into narrow strips. Place one tablespoon of the walnut mix on one end of the pastry strip and roll it up tightly into a small cylinder (see p.204). Repeat this process, until all the ingredients are used up. Place the prepared pieces of «kataifi» on a buttered pan and sprinkle them with melted butter. Bake in a medium oven for about 30 minutes. In the meantime, prepare the syrup as follows:

place the sugar, the water, the lemon juice and the lemon rind in a pot and boil them for 15 minutes over a medium fire. When the pieces of «kataifi» are ready, pour the boiling syrup over them, while they are still hot.

Káyk me Kerássia

CAKE WITH CHERRIES

Bring the butter to room temperature and beat it in the mixer. While continuing to beat, successively mix in the sugar, the eggs, the vanilla, the baking powder and the milk. Next, gradually add the flour and the cherries. Butter and flour a cake tin and pour in the batter. Make sure the tin is only 3/4 full so that the batter does not spill over the edges, as it rises. Bake in a moderate oven for about 20 minutes having only the bottom elements lit. Continue to bake for another 35-40 minutes with both the lower and upper elements lit. When the cake cools down, remove it from the tin and garnish it with whipped cream and preserved cherries.

- ◇ 200 grams (7 oz) butter
- ◇ 1 ½ teacups sugar
- ◇ 4 eggs
- ◇ 2 teacups flour
- ◇ 3/4 teacup milk
- ◇ 1 teacup finely chopped preserved cherry
- ◇ 2 envelopes vanilla (powder)
- ◇ 1 teaspoon baking powder

THE OLIVE AND OIL IN GREECE

The olive tree is the blessed tree of the Greeks and its fruit has been an irreplaceable, daily food since ancient times. Olive oil, on the other hand, is a basic ingredient of the Greek cuisine and can be found in almost every household, at such an extend that the word "olive oil" is synonymous with the world "oil". The Greeks, accustomed for centuries to using olive oil, have realized its considerable advantages over the other kinds of oil of vegetable origin and have the top position in the per capita consumption all over the world. A factor which contributes to the superior tasty quality of the Greek cuisine is the use of pure olive oil. Therefore, the cultivation of the olive tree is of a special financial and social interest, since thousands of Greek families, mainly of the southern and island part of the country, base their economy exclusively on it. On a world scale, Greece is second in the production of edible olives and third in the production of olive oil.

CULTIVATION OF OLIVE TREES IN ANCIENT TIMES

The primitive phases of cultivating olive trees in the area of the Aegean are obscure. However, excavations of Neolithic settlements have many times brought to light charred olive tree trunks. The domestication of the olive tree dates back to the early Bronze Age (3rd millennium BC), but the systematic exploitation of the olive tree started in Crete during the 2nd millennium BC. Representations of olive trees as well as olives, olive presses and storing oil vessels found on the island date back to the Minoan Age, after 1700 BC. The findings show that the people of the Minoan Age used olives in their diet and oil as a fuel. It seems that the wealth of the Minoan Crete was partly based on oil export.

The importance of the cultivation of olive trees and of oil for the economy of the Cretan- Mycenaean society became widely known for the first time through the deciphering of the linear b'. Numerous earthen tablets from Knossos, Mycenae, Pylos and other Mycenaean palaces are engraved with the syllable-symbols of linear b' for the olive tree (e-ra-wa), oil (e-ra-wo) and the olive. At the same time, the same tablets show the ideogrammatic pictures of the olive tree and its products. Oil was one of the most important products of Greece not only during the prehistoric era but also during all the phases of its history. According to the Greek mythology, the olive tree was a gift of the Gods: Athena, the goddess, offered the olive tree to the Athenians and so she became their protector. As the ancient writers teach us,

the cultivation of olive trees was intensively practiced all over Greece. Solon, the wise lawmaker of the 6th century BC, defined the ideal distance between two olive trees so that the biggest possible crop would be provided and also forbade cutting more than two trees per year. Apart from the financial importance that the cultivation of olive trees had, due to the considerable export of oil to many ancient countries, the Greeks used olive oil for treating purposes, as a lighting means, in their religious ceremonies and in the painting of walls and vessels. Above all,

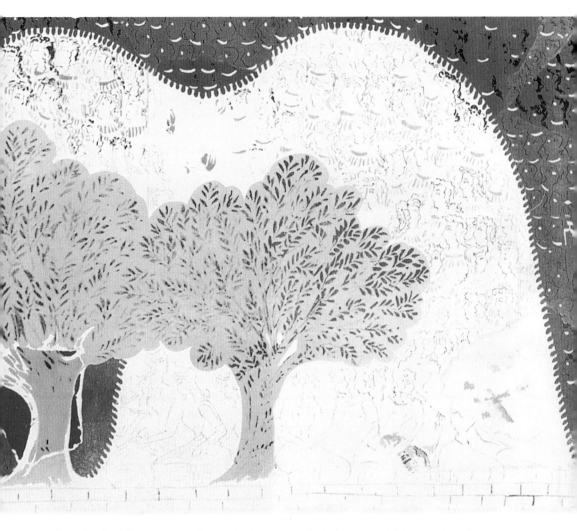

though, the olive tree was the symbol of peace, wisdom and victory.

The winners of the Olympic Games received as a prize a wreath made of the branch of an olive tree, symbol of peace and reconciliation of the people. In Athens, as well, the olive tree was associated with the prize of similar athletic games, a prize which did not have only a symbolic value but was accompanied by a considerable financial reward. Every four years, the Athenians organized in their city the famous Panathenaea, a festive event which included religious ceremonies and athletic games, in honour of Athena. The winners of the games were awarded big earthen vessels, the famous Panathenean urns, which were full of olive oil. These luxurious urns, which today are exhibited in many museums of the world, were decorated with representations of athletic games and of the goddess Athena. Each winner -mainly of the harness racing- could receive from 30 to 70 urns containing 2.5 up to 5 tons of oil from the sacred olive tree fields of the city. It seems that the winners could sell the awarded oil, as it is deduced by the big quantity of Panathenean urns found all over the Mediterranean up to the Peninsula of Crimea. As it is mentioned, with the money from the selling of the oil, they could buy 2-3 houses or 140 sheep!

During the Roman years, the Greek production of olives and oil was still of particular importance for the Greeks and the exports of the valuable product brought considerable profits. A similar activity was affirmed for the Byzantine period. In addition, with Christianity prevailing, the olive tree acquired a special symbolic importance for the new religion. Noah's pigeon carried an olive branch, a sign of God's mercy, and Christ himself called the olive tree "a blessed tree". Every Christian is anointed with oil, burns candles, products of olive oil, and continues to light their candles using oil in the icon stand of the Greek household. Moreover, in Athos, the main monastery complex of Greece, the cultivation of olive trees has been systematically practiced since the 10th century. In many monasteries of Mount Athos the traditional oil presses have been kept providing a clear picture of the pre-industrial and early industrial technology.

◁ p. 209
Relief wall-painting found in the Knossos palace (c.1500 BC).

MODERN PRODUCTION

Nowadays, the cultivation of olive trees and oil production is practiced in Greece using modern mechanical means. The species under cultivation is Olea Europea, the main characteristic of which is its longevity. In the Mediterranean, there are olive trees hundreds of years old still producing fruit. In Kalamata, there is an olive tree 800 years old with trunk diameter and height 8 meters, which has been declared as a natural monument of the area. On Iera Odos of Athens there was, until recently, the historical "Plato's olive tree", which according to the tradition was planted by the great Greek philosopher and consequently was 2,500 years old!

The olive tree grows in arid areas, even on stony or rocky soil. In fertile and well-irrigated soil it bears fruit and grows very quickly but it cannot stand temperatures lower than -9° C. The harvesting of the olives is done when they are in the final stage of ripeness, the so-called stage of "industrial ripeness", when the colour changes from green-yellow to black. If the harvesting is done earlier, the yield in olive oil is small and not of good quality, while if it is delayed, the fruit loses in weight and volume and oil acidity increases.

In the past, the harvesting of the olives was done exclusively by hand after the fruit falling on the ground. In order to facilitate this method, nowadays plastic nets are spread on the ground from which the olives should be gathered within approximately fifteen days. The harvesting is often done with thrashing the olive tree but efforts are being made to abandon this method in order not to hurt the olive fruit. For this reason mechanical means of harvesting as well as chemical preparations which facilitate the falling of the fruit from the tree are used in recent times. After the gathering, the olives are stored for a small period of time in bags or crates and are transported to oil presses. There they take out the leaves and wash the fruit and afterwards put them in the oil mill: two or three cylindrical or cone granite stones rotating around a metal or wooden axis crashing olives. The pugging of the fruit follows in special machines/ equipment which separate the oil from the plant juices and the procedure is concluded in the oil press where the olive oil is removed from the olive pulp. For this last stage nowadays the hydraulic press is used, which has brought a real revolution in the field of oil production.

According to data of the International Congress of Olive Oil, Greece is the third olive oil producing country in the world (16% of the global production) but it still holds the first position worldwide in the export of excellent pure olive oil in bulk. The supremacy in quality of the Greek olive oil is mainly due to the favourable climatic conditions of the country and the experience of thousand of years in cultivating olive trees. A especially important part in maintaining this superior quality is played by the distribution of the Greek olive tree fields to numerous small farmers who use pure, traditional methods of cultivation. 120 million olive trees in the country are today cultivated by 350,000 families who use approximately 3,000 oil presses for the extraction of oil. Moreover, the standard olive oil of the state guarantees a quality which is in accordance with the European specifications. Good olive oil is easily distinguished by its transparent colour, its taste and fragrance, which should be similar to the one of the olive immediately after the gathering. Acidity comes up to a percentage of 1% to 3.3%.

In the past decade, the nourishing value of olive oil in relation to other kinds of oil has been more widely known. Its balanced composition in saturated and unsaturated oily acids guarantees good health. Pediatrics recognizes it as an important factor for the balance of metabolism and brain and bone development, while it is recommended for elderly people because its vitamin E slows down cell alteration and, consequently, natural aging. Olive oil also contributes to the prevention of ulcer and gall ailments whereas due to its monosaturated olivary acid, it reduces cholesterol, the increase of which leads to heart and vascular ailments and arteriosclerosis. Moreover, olive oil is the unique kind of oil which needs only mechanical means for its extraction. In all the rest the composition of which is similar to the one of petrol!

The fruit of olive oil is, of course, of similar nourishing value and it constitutes a tasty appetizer, a basic element of the daily diet of the Greeks. However, olives in Greece are consumed mainly raw and are rarely used in cooking. They are gathered at the end of the year, at the same time with the gathering of the olives for oil. There is a big variety of edible olives which depends on the area the fruit comes from and its way of processing. The most famous are the olives of Kalamata and Amphissa. The ways of processing and preservation are not very much different from the methods used in antiquity.

THE GREEK CHEESE

Cheese is another product which is unbreakably linked with the Greek cuisine and is almost always found on the daily menu either as an appetizer or accompanying the main dishes or as a basic ingredient or complement of many kinds of food (pies, salads, saganaki -fried cheese- pasta, omelets, sandwiches). The knowledge of how to curdle cheese from milk comes from ancient times; it seems that today there is a similar process all over Greece. The Greeks produce a great variety of cheeses, most of which are of home origin, while some are of foreign origin but produced in Greece. Moreover, despite the considerable home production, Greece imports cheese from many foreign countries. Greece is in addition the first country in Europe in the consumption of cheese per person, a fact which is mainly due to the popularity of the Greek cheese feta.

More generally, cheeses are divided into hard and soft ones. The soft ones are prepared after a brief treatment, they retain water in their mass and mature more quickly. Their disadvantage is that they cannot be kept for long, only in very special conditions or in the fridge. The hard cheeses need a more prolonged treatment, contain a very small percentage of water, mature slowly, but can be kept for a long time. Let us see analytically the different kinds of Greek cheeses.

A. SOFT CHEESES

Feta: the most famous Greek cheese, with the biggest consumption in the country. It is white and is made from sheep milk. It has a semi sour, salty taste and is kept in barrels or tins with salt water. It is a necessary ingredient of the famous village salad, but it can also be served as a tasty appetizer served raw with oil, oregano and pepper or grilled with tomato and oregano. It accompanies wonderfully the so called veg-

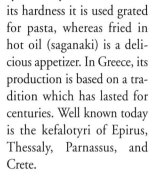

etable dishes while it is used as the main ingredient of the traditional cheese pie.

Telemes: a kind of feta cheese made from cow's milk with a whitish colour. It is cut in small pieces and kept in vessels with salt.

Manouri: white cheese made from whey with a big quantity of fatty goat or sheep milk or cream. Unsalted, very rich in butter. It is kept for a small period of time but it is very tasty and of superior quality. The manouri of Thrace, Macedonia, Epirus, Naxos and Crete is well known.

Myzithra: white cheese made from whey. It belongs to the same category as manouri, but its quality is inferior. It is served fresh or dry in which case it is mainly used grated for pasta. The Myzithra of Crete is very famous. They make very tasty small pies with myzithra, salty or sweet.

Anthotyro: a kind of very soft myzithra with a high content in butter. It is often produced completely skimmed. The anthotyro of Crete and the Cyclades is quite famous.

Kopanisti: spicy cheese made from fat sheep milk in which salt and pepper is added. It is extremely soft and is served spread on bread, offered as an appetizer for wine or ouzo.

B. HARD CHEESES

Kefalotyri: white yellow cheese from a mixture of sheep and goat milk. It has small holes and a spicy and salty taste. Because of its hardness it is used grated for pasta, whereas fried in hot oil (saganaki) is a delicious appetizer. In Greece, its production is based on a tradition which has lasted for centuries. Well known today is the kefalotyri of Epirus, Thessaly, Parnassus, and Crete.

Kefalograviera: white yellow cheese made from cow's milk or from a mixture of sheep and cow's milk. It has a slightly spicy taste and many small holes.

Graviera: semi-hard yellow cheese made from cow's milk or from cow's milk and a small quantity of sheep milk. It is similar to kefalograviera but it has a sweeter taste and bigger holes.

Kasseri: semi-hard, white-yellow cheese made from sheep milk with a slightly spicy taste. The production of kasseri in Central Greece is quite important.

GREEK WINES

Wine is the main drink associated with food. A good meal is accompanied most of the times with the appropriate wine, necessary for a complete savoury pleasure. Quite often, a delicious meal does not come to our expectations, if it is not consumed accompanied by a glass of wine. So, knowing which kind of wine goes with which dish is extremely important. Following a general rule, we could say that light wines are associated with light cooking, whereas strong and spicy tastes need heavier kinds of wine.

As far as the Greek cuisine is concerned, appetizers are combined with dry white wine, as well as sea food and fish, which in addition need a fine, subtle fragrance; if sea food dishes have stronger taste, the best accompaniment is retsina (resinated wine) or a soft rose wine. Red wine is unique for meat, light or not, depending on how spicy the taste of the meal is. Dry white wine goes better with pasta and vegetables, rose or red wine with omelets and red or dry rose wine with rice dishes. Generally speaking, what defines the kind of wine we are going to select for a meal is the spiciest dish on our table.

Besides its usage as an accompaniment of a good meal, wine is an unrivalled means for the facilitation of human communication. In a controlled degree, wine drinking is a relaxation means and leads to the creation of a joyful atmosphere and fun. Moreover, apart from very few contra-indications- mainly in cases of extreme consumption, wine offers an invigorating effect to the organism, stimulates the activity of all the organs and shows antitoxic, anti-septic and bactericide action. When consumed in medium quantities, it increases longevity and contributes to the cure of numerous ailments.

WINE PRODUCTION IN ANTIQUITY

The benefits offered by wine have been known since very old times, as it is shown by references in mythology and by the archaeological findings of ancient peoples. It appears that vineyards producing grapes for wine were first cultivated in Central Asia and from there, they were spread in the Middle East. The Greeks were one of the oldest peoples which practiced vine cultivation and wine production and indeed the spread of wine in many areas of the Mediterranean was due to their commerce.

According to the Greek mythology, the Greeks learned the cultivation of vines from Dionysus, who became the God protector of wine and, generally, of vegetation and fertility. Son of Zeus and Selene, daughter of the king Cadmus of Thebes, Dionysus was chased by the wife of Zeus, Hera, and took refuge in a wild mountain, where he was brought up by the Nymphs inside a cave full of wild vines. When he grew up, the wrath of Hera forced him to wander all over the world where he started teaching without stopping whatever he knew about vines and wine. In his wanderings the Nymphs Maenads and a numerous group of Satyrs followed him. The Maenads held sticks decorated with ivy and vine leaves and fell into ecstasy dancing in a frantic way. The Satyrs, monstrous beings, forest spirits, participated in the bustling team running, dancing and chasing the Nymphs. The God with his entourage offered the people who welcomed him his sweet wine in order to enjoy themselves and find comfort. Those, however, who did not accept him were severely punished because he could induce mania with his wine and lead them to extremities. From the myths that have come down to us, the double nature of the God and of the wine itself is evident. When wine drinking is mild and controlled, man is led to a unique psychological uplift. However, when wine is consumed without any measure and control, it can lead to a disastrous mania. Dionysus taught the mortals the correct use of its gifts and punished those that refused them or went over the allowed limits. Most of the

Greek regions adopted the cultivation of vine and worshipped the God, since through intoxication and the frenzied dance, people could free themselves from the daily worries and experience a feeling of unlimited freedom.

According to archaeological testimonies, vines were cultivated for the first in the region of Northern Greece during the 4th millennium BC while it has been ascertained with certainty that wine was produced during the 2nd millennium BC. Homer mentions the numerous kinds of wine and praises it not only as a pleasant drink but as a medicine as well. Hesiod describes different ways of wine making. The sure thing is that ancient Greeks promoted wine making in a very high degree. Every city could present its own wines, while the most famous ones were the ones of Thassos, Chios, Cos, Rhodes, Euboea, Thera, Crete, Cyprus, Mytelene, Naxos and Thrace.

The wines that the Greeks loved most were the strong and sweet wines with many spices (cinnamon, thyme etc). At the same time they used to make wine from apples (cider), pears (*apitis*), quince (*kydonitis*), figs (*sykitis*) and pomegranates (*roditis*). Quite often, they would pour some sea water in the wine, because they believed that this was a way to preserve it for a longer period of time. For exactly the same reason, they would add pieces of pine bark creating thus the most famous Greek wine up to now, retsina (resinated Greek wine). The wine prepared in this way was kept in earthenware jars or in special big urns in which they exported it as well. The handholds of the urns were stamped confirming the capacity, quality, age, and origin of the product. Other vessels associated with wine were the following: the skinbag, the *kantharos* -the characteristic cup of Dionysus- cups (kylikes, skyfoi), wine pumps for pumping wine from bigger vessels and craters, big vessels for mixing wine with water.

In antiquity, wine was drunk not only by men and elderly people but by women and children as well. However, contrary to modern customs, they never consumed it if it was not mixed beforehand with water (wine mixed- oinos kekramenos). The ratio at Hesiod's time (7th century BC) was 3 parts water to one part wine. Moreover, the way of drinking was different from the modern one. During the symposia, for example, the main dish was not accompanied by wine. Wine drinking followed afterwards combined with sweet desserts, the so called "tragemata" (dry fruit, almonds, honey pies). The ancient Greeks did not seem to praise excessive consumption of wine and intoxication. As it is mentioned in a poem of Anakreontas:

"I fill only three craters with wine and water for the wise ones.
The one, the first one, they drink for their health,
The second one for the sake of love and pleasure

The third one to sleep;
And when the wise guests drink that one too,
They go home.
The fourth one is not for me any more
Because it brings foul language and fights
Whereas the fifth one quarrels and noise..."

During the symposia, the participants used to discuss philosophical issues for hours on end on a topic of their own choice. It is not accidental, that Plato compiled his most famous philosophical dialogues drinking wine in symposia. He writes: "Wine reconciles you with yourself".

In Roman years, there was wine galore during the luxurious banquets of the Roman state officials and in many different varieties coming from a number of enslaved countries of the empire. The same happened in the huge Byzantine state in which there was special preference for the wine from the Greek islands. Vine cultivation was always practiced in Greece even during the Turkish occupation. Although the Islamic religion considers wine consumption a sin for the Muslims, it permitted it for the enslaved Greeks on the condition that they would pay 13% of the wine production as a tax.

All over the Greek territory, we can see some remnants of the places or the vessels used for wine production during the past centuries: cavities in the soil, potholes of rocks, earthenware vessels, wooden wine presses ("linoi") or built ones, big tanks -all witnesses of older times during which vine harvest or grape crushing reached the dimensions of folk frenzy. Today wine presses are automated and wineries constitute a kind of industrial facility -a fact easily justified, if one takes into consideration the huge production and wine consumption world wide.

MODERN PRODUCTION

Modern Greece seems to continue a history of thousands of years in wine production since vine cultivation is practiced all over the Greek territory. 200,000 families are involved in this practice which produces approximately 0.5 billion litres of wine in a total of 360 wineries. A big part of this production is exported abroad and is considered to be of a particularly good quality. According to the world rules, approximately 20 Greek territories produce wines with the label "Appellation of Higher Quality". The variety of Greek wines is very big due to the intense variations in the morphology of the soil from area to area. Indicatively we mention some of the most important varieties which are produced in the Greek territory.

THRACE- MACEDONIA:

Thrace, the most famous area in antiquity for producing the famous wine of Thassos, produces today restricted varieties which are inferior to those of other areas. Macedonia, though, has produced some of the most remarkable Greek wines.

Naousa: deep red, rich wine from the Xynomavro variety, at the mountainsides of Vermio.

Amyntaio: light red and rose wine of the Xynomavro variety.

Goumenissa: light flavoured red wine of the Xynomavro and Negoska varieties on Paiko mountain .

Plagies Melitona: red and white wine from a combination of the French varieties Cabernet Sauvignon and Cabernet Franc and the Greek Limnio variety.

Topikos Agioritikos: red and white wine produced at the monasteries of Mount Athos. The tradition of wine making of Mount Athos started in the 10th century BC with the establishment of the first monasteries of the peninsula as wine was the basic ingredient of the monks' diet and it was also used as a therapeutical means.

EPIRUS:

Zitsa: at the namesake village northwest of Ioannina, light dry white wine with a fruity fragrance of the Debina variety.

Metsovo: at the namesake area, red, rich

wine of the Cabernet Sauvignon variety.

IONIAN ISLANDS

Robola of Cefallenia: of the namesake variety, excellent dry white wine.

Mavrodafne and Moschato of Cefallenia: two particularly sweet wines from the island.

Vertzani: red wine from Lefkada.

THESSALY

Rapsani: northeast of Olympus, high quality red fine wine of the Xynomavro, Stavroto and Krasato varieties.

Agchialou: from the namesake area, light white wine of the Rodites and Savatiano varieties.

CENTRAL GREECE

The Savatiano grapes are cultivated most of all in the areas of Attica, Euboea and Voiotia. This variety produces the famous Retsina with a finer aroma than the one of the retsina of ancient times. A big variety of white wines are also produced in Attica.

THE PELOPONNESE

The richest area in wine production in Greece.

Nemea: from the namesake area among the vineyards of Corinth, deep red wine, which has taken the name "Hercules's blood" because of its colour, with a rich fragrance of the Aghiorgitiko variety.

Mantinia: from the vineyards of Central Peloponnese, high quality of dry white wine with a fine aroma and fruity taste of the Moschofilero and Asproudes variety.

Mavrodaphne of Patras: sweet wine of the Mavrodaphne variety and black Corinthian dry grapes. Muscat of Patras: sweet white wines with fine aroma of the Muscat variety.

Dry white wine of Patras: of the Rodites variety, at the slopes of the Panahaiko mountain.

EASTERN AEGEAN ISLANDS

Samos: renowned sweet, aromatic wines of the white Muscat variety which is cultivated at various altitudes, up to 800 m.

Lemnos: 1. traditional light red wine originating from ancient times of the Limnio variety and 2. dry or sweet white wine of the Muscat of Alexandria variety.

CYCLADES

Santorini: the soil of the island of Thera, unique due to its volcanic composition, allows the cultivation of Asyrtiko variety which produces a high quality white wine. A sweet white wine, Visanto, is also produced.

Paros: strong red wine with velvet taste of the white Monemvasia and red Mandilaria varieties.

DODECANESE

Rhodes: 1. dry white wine of the Athiri variety, 2. red wine of the Mandilaria variety, 3. Muschat wine of the namesake variety.

CRETE

Sitia: on the eastern side of the island, dry red wine of the Liatiko variety.

Daphnes: the same wine as that of Sitia of the Liatiko variety; it has been cultivated since ancient times. Also, sweet wine of the same variety.

Maltzavias: sweet wine of the Liatiko variety, from Heraklion.

Archanes: dry red wine of the Mandilaria and Kotsifali varieties.

Peza: 1. dry red wine of the Mandilaria and Kotsifali varieties, 2. dry white of the Vilana variety, 3. rose of the Rozaki variety.

USEFUL ADVICE

Cooking is artistry. It needs imagination and a good mood.

Before you start cooking, read the recipe carefully.

Follow the instructions as well as the order that you will use the ingredients.

Vegetables must be fresh because that's how food becomes tastier. As vegetables and fragrant plants lose their freshness easily, put them in a plastic food bag before storing them in the fridge.

Use all kinds of vegetables, raw or boiled, to make salads or to garnish the main dish.

Do not boil vegetables for long. This way all their vitamins will be retained.

In order to preserve the fragrance of herbs and seeds, add them into your food shortly before cooking is complete.

Prefer pure olive oil. It is healthier and makes food tastier.

Programme your menu on a weekly basis. This way you will have quality in your diet and save time and money.

INDEX